Kinaesthetic Learning in Early Childhood

Strongly grounded in research and rich with practical examples for educators, this book demonstrates the importance and benefits of kinaesthetic learning in young children's learning and development.

Kinaesthetic or hands-on active learning is extremely important for young children's personal, social and cultural development. Without this kind of learning children may be at risk of poor behaviour, social development and academic learning outcomes. This book shares concrete examples of authentic kinaesthetic learning experiences, across different discipline areas, in a range of Early Childhood contexts. The chapters outline practical approaches to kinaesthetic learning in the classroom to help educators to engage young children, covering curriculum areas such as the arts, mathematics, literacy, digital technologies and English as a foreign language. These practical examples are supported by a range of research and theories related to the benefits of kinaesthetic learning for young children, as well as authentic classroom data.

Written by leading experts in the field, this book shares authentic, appropriate classroom strategies for implementing kinaesthetic learning with young children and will be essential reading for researchers as well as pre- and in-service educators.

Georgina Barton is a professor of literacies and pedagogy at the University of Southern Queensland, Brisbane, Australia. Before being an academic, Georgina taught in schools for over 20 years including teaching English in South India. She has been an acting principal and a lead teacher in the areas of literacy and numeracy. Georgina also has extensive experience in teaching the arts in schools and universities and often utilises the arts to support students' literacy learning outcomes.

T0373567

Susanne Garvis is a professor at the School of Education and Professional Studies at Griffith University. She is a specialist in Early Childhood Education and has been involved with many national and international projects around policy, quality and learning with young children. Her most recent was a large meta-analysis exploring teacher qualifications and environmental quality. She has worked in many countries and currently lives in Australia.

Kinaesthetic Learning in Early Childhood

Exploring Theory and Practice for Educators

Edited by
Georgina Barton and Susanne Garvis

Routledge
Taylor & Francis Group
LONDON AND NEW YORK

Designed cover image: © Getty Images

First published 2024
by Routledge
4 Park Square, Milton Park, Abingdon, Oxon OX14 4RN

and by Routledge
605 Third Avenue, New York, NY 10158

Routledge is an imprint of the Taylor & Francis Group, an informa business

British Library Cataloguing-in-Publication Data
A catalogue record for this book is available from the British Library

Library of Congress Cataloging-in-Publication Data
Names: Barton, Georgina, editor. | Garvis, Susanne, editor.
Title: Kinaesthetic learning in early childhood: exploring theory and practice for educators / edited by Georgina Barton and Susanne Garvis.
Other titles: Kinesthetic learning in early childhood
Description: Abingdon, Oxon; New York, NY : Routledge, 2023. |
Includes bibliographical references and index. |
Identifiers: LCCN 2022061086 (print) | LCCN 2022061087 (ebook) |
ISBN 9781032215198 (hardback) | ISBN 9781032215181 (paperback) |
ISBN 9781003268772 (ebook)
Subjects: LCSH: Early childhood education–Activity programs. | Active learning.
Classification: LCC LB1139.35.A37 K58 2023 (print) |
LCC LB1139.35.A37 (ebook) | DDC 372.21–dc23/eng/20230208
LC record available at https://lccn.loc.gov/2022061086
LC ebook record available at https://lccn.loc.gov/2022061087

ISBN: 9781032215198 (hbk)
ISBN: 9781032215181 (pbk)
ISBN: 9781003268772 (ebk)

DOI: 10.4324/9781003268772

Typeset in Optima
by Newgen Publishing UK

We dedicate this book to all children who crave play-based and kinaesthetic learning in their everyday lives.

Contents

Contents

Contributors

Katrina Allegos is an early childhood teacher with a passion for developing strong relationships with learners and their families, setting children up to develop confident dispositions for learning. Katrina has worked in a variety of roles including as a lead teacher, support teacher and educator. Katrina currently works as a teacher's assistant in the pre-prep group at Fintona Girl's School Early Learning Centre.

Marc Angelier is (since 2019), with Marie Oddoux, in charge of the development and implementation of the inclusive LEGO Braille Bricks concept for the LEGO Foundation. He is a staunch defender of braille, co-author of tactile books for blind children and specialised teaching methods, and travels the world training teachers in pedagogical techniques specific to visual impairment to make inclusive schooling for all a reality! He participates in research studies and training programmes to increase students with disabilities' accessibility to education. This amazing concept allows visually impaired children from all over the world to learn braille and develop the breadth of skills they will need for the future.

Melissa Cain is a senior lecturer and head of secondary education at Australian Catholic University's Brisbane campus. Melissa's teaching and research focuses on initial teacher education, inclusive education and creative pedagogies with a current focus on supporting equitable participation for students with blindness and low vision in mainstream schools. Prior to working in higher education, Melissa was a schoolteacher in Australia and Southeast Asia. She has managed three large-scale national Learning and Teaching projects and has produced an international MOOC through

EdX and Microsoft. Melissa has received several higher education teaching awards and is the recipient of the Callaway Doctoral Award.

Susan Chapman is a lecturer in the Faculty of Creative Industries, Education and Social Justice at the Queensland University of Technology. She has worked professionally as an actor and musician, teaching the arts in primary, secondary and tertiary sectors. Her research focus is on arts immersion pedagogy, professional learning and STEAM.

Anna Crozier is a teacher of three-year-olds at Fintona Girls School in Melbourne, Australia. Anna has taught in London and Australia in all sectors of early childhood and primary education and has over 20 years of experience. Anna is passionate about all aspects of Early Childhood Education and development and takes pride in being an accomplice to each child's learning journey.

Helen Darrer is currently a K3 co-teacher in the Early Learning Centre at Fintona Girl's School in Melbourne, Australia. She has been a member of staff for the past 14 years. Helen has participated in the advanced study tour at the Loris Malaguzzi Centre in Reggio Emilia, Italy and is inspired by this approach to the education of young children.

Nicole Delaney is a lecturer in Early Childhood Education at the University of Southern Queensland. Prior to this, Nicole gained experience as an Early Years teacher in regional Early Childhood and primary settings. Her research interests are located within the broader Early Childhood field with specific interests in arts-based practices, early mathematical thinking and social inclusion. Nicole is an advocate for children's voices.

Jackie Dimattina is Early Learning Centre Curriculum and Operations Leader at Fintona Girl's School in Melbourne, Australia. She has over 20 years of teaching experience in New Zealand, London and Australia. Jackie has participated in the advanced study tour at the Loris Malaguzzi Centre in Reggio Emilia, Italy and is passionate about this approach to Early Childhood Education.

Suzanne Donaghey is a diploma-qualified educator with 20 years of experience in Early Childhood. Her interest in the Reggio approach enables children to learn through the natural environment and experience the joy of making discoveries and investigations within the programme.

Melissa Fanshawe is a senior lecturer in the School of Education at the University of Southern Queensland, Australia, specialising in mathematics curriculum and pedagogy. She has over 20 years of experience within Queensland schools as a teacher, advisory teacher, deputy and principal. In the tertiary space, Melissa is passionate about student success and access to education. Melissa is Vision Australia's education ambassador for the LEGO foundation's inclusive LEGO Braille Bricks.

Catherine Farrar holds a bachelor's degree in early childhood and primary education. She is a passionate educator with a focus on encapsulating the Reggio Emilia approach in her learning environments. Catherine actively recognises and differentiates her teaching environment to honour the unique learning needs of her students.

Wendy Goff is a senior lecturer and academic director in the School of Education at RMIT University. Wendy's research focuses on adult relationships and how they facilitate children's learning. She uses Early Childhood mathematics as one of the vehicles to study these relationships.

Amy Goodale is an early childhood teacher at Fintona Girl's School in Melbourne, Australia. Over the past 20 years, she has worked in the early childhood profession in both education and healthcare settings. Amy is passionate about family-centred practice and supporting positive infant and child mental health.

Heidi Harju-Luukkainen is a professor who works at Tampere University, University of Jvyäskylä (Finland) and Nord University (Norway). She has published more than 200 scholarly papers and has participated in more than 30 projects globally. Heidi has worked in multiple countries in high-level research universities (UCLA, USC), as well as in many Nordic research universities (HU, JYU, GU, NORD). She has developed education programmes for universities and has been a PI of PISA sub-assessments in Finland.

Charmian Harris is an early childhood teacher and a bachelor of education (EC and Primary). Her interest in the Reggio Emilia approach sets the foundation for enabling children to be leaders and co-constructors in their learning journey. Charmian advocates for the "independent thinker" enabling children to discover learning holistically, catering for diverse learners and supporting learning through connection.

Per Havgaard is a team lead at the LEGO Foundation. With over 20 years' experience in education and management, he is always leading, teaching and engaging with quality, passion and creativity. Constantly striving to facilitate environments where children can reach their full potential.

Jonna Kangas has a doctorate in education, is an adjunct professor, a university lecturer and a joint research member in the Playful Learning Center, Faculty of Education Science, University of Helsinki. Her research focus is on play-based pedagogy. She seeks to understand children's learning processes through joy and participation, and she uses her findings for designing innovative teacher training and mentoring programmes in Finland and developing countries. She is a director of the blended teacher training programme at the University of Helsinki.

Anh Hai Le has a doctorate in tertiary hospitality education from Griffith University. Her research interest focuses on curriculum development in tertiary education, with a particular interest in the process of building knowledge through scholarly engagement with industry in mix-sector higher education institutions. She has diverse experience, in teaching and curriculum development, across various disciplines in the higher education sector.

Monique Mandarakas is a casual lecturer at the University of Southern Queensland. She currently works in both Australia and the Netherlands. Monique returned to university later in life with a passion for social justice in education, aiming to make learning accessible for all. Monique comes from both an early childhood and primary teaching background. Her research interests have included supporting indigenous primary mathematics learning, parent and family engagement in education and the support of pre-service teachers. Most recently Monique has gained international experience playing an integral role in the development of the first bilingual public school in Eindhoven, The Netherlands.

Marie Oddoux is an occupational therapist specialising in braille and low vision. With more than 20 years of experience in the field of blindness, she wrote books for children and inclusive methods to learn through touch. Marie is a strong advocate for Braille and travels the world on training missions, particularly on inclusive education and visual impairment. She believes in the power of play, of learning through play for all children! Since 2019, with Marc Angelier, she has been in charge of the creation and implementation of the global LEGO Braille Bricks inclusive educational concept for the LEGO Foundation.

Georgie O'Meara is a bachelor of education, specialising in Early Childhood Education. Georgie is passionate about play-based education in the early years and takes great inspiration from the Reggio Emilia approach to learning. Currently, Georgie teaches in a pre-prep programme, where children's wellbeing is at the forefront.

Rebecca Trimble-Roles is a passionate, enthusiastic and highly experienced educator and leader in her field, with over 20 years of experience. She has been a principal of a multi-age school and a literacy and numeracy coach and mentor in independent schools. She has presented both state and nationwide on current trends in technology, literacy and numeracy across the curriculum.

Michelle Turner is a lecturer in Early Childhood Education at the School of Education at the University of Southern Queensland. She is currently the Early Years Specialist Convenor, advising programme directors around current developments in curriculum and pedagogy as well as ACECQA guidelines and quality assurance. Her PhD research was around the impact of reform on Early Childhood educators' professional practices. This investigation has led to research into teacher wellbeing. Michelle is currently working on a project that seeks to understand how initial teacher education programmes support pre-service teachers to improve the wellbeing experiences of Early Childhood Education and Care for young children and their families.

Tuulikki Ukkonen-Mikkola has a PhD in education and is a senior lecturer in the Faculty of Education Science, University of Jyväskylä. She is the person in charge of ECE teacher training at the University of Jyväskylä. Her research focus is teachers' pedagogical expertise, professional development and the development of teacher training in higher education. She is a vice chairperson of the Early Childhood Education Association Finland.

Marthy Watson is a lecturer in curriculum and pedagogy at the University of Southern Queensland. Her teaching and research are focused on reflective practice through arts-based learning, drama education and learning through play in the early years. She is particularly committed to children's expressive learning and engagement through the arts. Marthy has worked on numerous research projects supporting culturally and linguistically diverse communities through arts practices. She strongly advocates for the arts and regularly presents at conferences and arts workshops in schools.

Marie White is a lecturer at the National School of Education at Australian Catholic University. Marie has a background in Early Childhood Education and Care, with experience in both teaching and leadership spanning more than 20 years. Marie's research primarily focuses on leadership in Early Childhood Education and Care – specifically on the ways that leadership is discursively produced. Through her research, Marie seeks to disrupt taken-for-granted understandings of leadership.

Bin Wu is a lecturer at Swinburne University of Technology. Her research interests include the sociology of education, educational theories and philosophies. She is especially interested in diverse cultural values and experiences, past and present and how these affect the lives people live. Her recent research projects in Early Childhood Education focus on international teaching and teachers' knowledge in the context of play-based learning.

Tina Yngvesson is a lecturer in Early Childhood Education at the University of Borås as well as a PhD research fellow in education at Nord University in Norway. Alongside various international and national research projects in early learning, child development and parental involvement in education, she also has a strong interest in the emergence of curriculum and the bridge between policy and praxis.

Acknowledgements

We would like to acknowledge all the blind peer reviewers for this book.

The importance of kinaesthetic learning for Early Childhood

Georgina Barton and
Susanne Garvis

Introduction

Early childhood is a critical period of development for young children, and it is therefore important for educators to know what approaches might benefit such development. Often referring to birth to eight years of age, Early Childhood and Care Education (ECCE) aims to support children's social and cultural development through carefully planned educational programs. As espoused by the United Nations Educational, Scientific and Cultural Organisation [UNESCO] (n.d.):

> The period from birth to eight years old is one of remarkable brain development for children and represents a crucial window of opportunity for education. UNESCO believes Early Childhood Care and Education (ECCE) that is truly inclusive is much more than just preparation for primary school. It can be the foundation for emotional wellbeing and learning throughout life and one of the best investments a country can make as it promotes holistic development, gender equality and social cohesion.
>
> (p. 1)

It is important to recognise that ECCE is responsible for best preparing children for school but also supports children's individual health and participation in life. As such, many researchers have heralded the importance of kinaesthetic learning for children's physical, psycho-physical

DOI: 10.4324/9781003268772-1

and ultimately, overall progress as they move through their first years of schooling. Kinaesthetic learning involves students actively engaged in movement or tactile aspects of learning. It involves multisensory learning environments as they assist children to learn deeply through the action of doing. There are many reasons offered in the research literature as to why it is important to embed kinaesthetic learning in Early Childhood settings. This book, therefore, shares a range of chapters focused on these benefits and the application of kinaesthetic learning for young children in different contexts.

What is kinaesthetic learning?

Kinaesthetic learning is when children are participating in some kind of physical or tactile activity rather than being passive listeners or viewers within learning spaces. Kinaesthetic learning can include movement and/or touch and it has been proven to be extremely beneficial for young children's learning and development.

Children learn through multiple means and activities that are carefully designed for positive outcomes for all. According to UNESCO, there are 12 principles underpinning quality education for children. These are active involvement, social participation, meaningful activities, relating new infor- mation to prior knowledge, being strategic, engaging in self-regulation and being reflective, restricting prior knowledge, aiming towards understanding rather than memorisation, helping students to transfer, taking time to prac- tice, developmental and individual differences and creating motivated learners. In thinking about many of these principles, movement or what we call kinaesthetic learning is a core component.

Why a book on kinaesthetic learning in Early Childhood?

Strong evidence suggests that due to the everyday pressures on teachers to perform and hence raise academic standards, important approaches to learning, such as kinaesthetic learning, have been minimalised. More static and teacher-led approaches have begun to predominate classrooms largely because of high-stakes testing and to some extent pressure from parents and the community, given poor reporting on teachers and schools. This is despite copious amounts of educational research pointing to the benefits of varied approaches to learning including those that are hands-on and tactile.

Approaches to kinaesthetic learning in Early Childhood Education

As mentioned above, kinaesthetic learning involves children in physical activity or events where they use all of their senses while learning. Kinaesthetic learning can involve moving the whole body or individual hands-on learning activities. This type of learning involves some kind of stimulation as central to the learning process. Processing by children can often be faster if their body is busy doing something besides focusing on specific material.

Some children are more attracted to active learning than others. This may mean they have more advanced hand-eye coordination, greater motor memory, and high energy levels. Further, children who have high creative skills and enjoy experimenting with others enjoy active learning. Can aesthetic learning help children to see how things work and recall information more accurately and quickly?

Different learning strategies that are kinaesthetic are offered in the literature. Many of these are highlighted in alternative approaches to education such as Montessori, Reggio Emilia and Dalcroze. For example, in Montessori education, active learning through the five senses is very much encouraged. A Montessori philosophy supports all children but recognises their differences and understands that many young children need regular movement. Reggio Emilia and Dalcroze understand that kinaesthetic learners need to use both small and large muscles to process information provided to them in the classroom. Moving the body through hands-on learning is essential for many children to succeed (Tranquillo, 2008).

In Reggio Emilia schools, movement is an important component of learning. Famously known for its "100 languages of learning and play", the Reggio Emilia approach involves kinaesthetic learning for all children through a democratic approach. Children are encouraged to discover and expand learning opportunities through natural materials. Such active learning results in improved self-expression, communication, problem-solving, and logical thinking.

Dalcroze Eurhythmics is "based on the premise that the human body is the source of all musical ideas. Physical awareness, or kinaesthetic intelligence, is one of our most powerful senses" (Dalcroze Australia, n.d.).

Some other examples of kinaesthetic learning include having students stand while they flex their muscles and internalise information, which can help improve comprehension focus and retention. Another approach is using small movements to help children focus, which is particularly beneficial for students who find it difficult to sit still. Teachers can also help children by building exercise into their everyday activities as these have a positive effect on mental capacity. Other approaches can involve hands-on activities where children highlight text or use flashcards and engage in art activities including drawing, painting, mind mapping and storyboarding. It may also be useful to have students use the technique of tension and relaxation to help them focus on work. This also encourages healthy minds and bodies. Teachers can also use role play, when they act out ideas or concepts, and children can also use drama and movement to assist understanding.

Sutapa and Suharjana (2019) led an experimental study that aimed to identify the effect of kinaesthetic learning on children's gross motor skills. Their study involved 28 girls and 40 boys aged 5–6 years. Two different groups of children received different types of activities, that is, kinaesthetic-based physical activity and contemporary treatment. The contemporary-based treatment was different to kinaesthetic movement as it only involved walking, running, jumping, throwing, kicking, crawling, and climbing not in a series of movements. The kinaesthetic movement included a 20-metre sprint, arm power by throwing a tennis ball, power legs with long jump without the start, balance by walking on a 4-metre-long beam, and agility with Illinois tests. The result of the study showed that both kinaesthetic and contemporary-based activities improved children's gross motor skills. There was a slight difference showing that the kinaesthetic-based physical activities are better for improving running ability, agility and balance, while the contemporary activities improved the ability to jump and throw a ball.

Benefits of kinaesthetic learning

Across the literature, kinaesthetic learning has been linked to benefits in other areas for young children. For example, a recent study reported that improving motor competence skills in young children benefits their executive function and numeracy skills (Hudson et al., 2020). Similar findings have also been made around the benefits of music and movement with early mathematics, with increased attention and enhanced understanding reported (Samsudin et al., 2019). As such, it suggests that kinaesthetic learning also has the potential to support the early development of all children and allow for skills to be supported and developed prior to schooling. Kinaesthetic learning could have the potential to support all children in elements of becoming ready for schooling and provide the building blocks for early cognitive development.

Kinaesthetic learning has also been considered important in Early Childhood Education for teaching foreign languages. This includes the focus on the Total Physical Response (TPR) method, which coordinates words with actions to teach through activity (Richards & Rodgers, 2001). This could include examples of songs, games, stories and actions to engage the attention of the young child through movement. Positive examples of the TPR approach have been reported by Sühendan (2013) with many benefits to support the emotional, physical, cognitive and language development of young children. Thus, the benefits of kinaesthetic learning in Early Childhood environments is extensive to support young children's learning.

Dance has also been reported in the literature as important to the development of young children (Deans et al., 2012; Deans, 2016; Wright, 2003). In a qualitative study, Deans (2016) reports that dance enabled young children to engage in thinking, imaginative problem-solving and aesthetic decision-making through multimodal semiotic meaning-making. The role of the teacher was important in supporting and enabling the learning associated with dance within the Early Years setting. Such research also provides clear arguments for the importance of movement in Early Years programs to support and contribute to children's learning and development.

Kinaesthetic learning activities have also been linked to increased handwriting in children (Harris & Livesey, 1992). In the study by Harris and Livesey (1992) with kindergarten and year one children with poor handwriting, engagement in kinaesthetic sensitivity practice improved handwriting performance. As such, it is important for teachers to consider kinaesthetic activities for improving motor skills and associated tasks with young children.

We have only touched on a handful of the benefits of kinaesthetic learning activities. However, there is clear evidence across the literature of the importance of kinaesthetic learning with young children. In this book, we will bring together evidence from different research projects to really help build the field further and provide examples for teachers of pedagogical practice.

How Early Childhood teachers might embed kinaesthetic learning in their classroom practice

Early childhood teachers can engage with kinaesthetic learning in a number of different ways, depending on the learning outcomes. This means if kinaesthetic learning will be used as the tool to achieve in other areas (in a form or integration activity such as to enhance mathematical understanding) or if improved and enhanced, kinaesthetic learning is the overarching goal (kinaesthetic activities to enhance kinaesthetic learning). For example, if the focus is on movement, Early Childhood teachers may create various challenges for children, with blocks for children to learn and increase hand manipulation. Alternatively, if the focus is on engineering, blocks can be used with kinaesthetic learning to support different principles around balance and supports with the blocks. A good question to consider is "what are my intentions for the child's learning?" The role of the teacher is then to consider what strategies and experience can be used to support the child's learning.

The role of the teacher is to also find a good balance for young children and to support them through child-initiated and teacher-led activities. This requires knowing the child and their interests and allowing the child to be supported in various environments with different resources to support kinaesthetic learning. For example, if a child is learning about different pitches in music, allowing children the opportunity to bang and hit different materials provides an opportunity for kinaesthetic learning. This teacher could consider placing different materials out for the child to explore and a range of different objects to hit the different materials (such as wood or plastic).

A key reflection is the use of Early Years planning to support embedding kinaesthetic learning in classroom practices. This would be either starting with an observation from the child and their interest and extending on it with a learning experience, or starting with a planned activity for the teacher that engages the child's interests and continues to scaffold and support as more observations of the child's learning is undertaken.

Planning for children's learning is cyclical and allows for continuous reflection, observation, planning, implementation and evaluation to support the learning experience. When teachers are engaged in planning cycles, they will be able to engage with kinaesthetic learning in the two ways mentioned above. They will know the child's learning and be able to look at how children's kinaesthetic learning can be supported in activities, routines, transitions, interactions, indoor and outdoor environments and investigations.

Overview of the book

Chapter 2 (Garvis, Barton and Le) starts the focus on kinaesthetic learning with a systematic review of literature with a PRISMA approach. Key themes emerge around the activities, age ranges and the developmental impact across the research literature. Research gaps also emerge and show further need for research that focuses on including planning, programming and the professional learning of kinaesthetic learning.

The next chapter (Chapter 3) by Yngvesson and Garvis explores two case studies in Australia and Sweden with a type of self-narrative. The authors unpack understanding of children's experiential learning from different perspectives, connecting and contrasting the two case studies within Early Childhood Education and Care.

The book next moves to Chapter 4 (Allegos, Crozier, Darrer, Dimattina, Donaghey, Farrar, Goodale, Harris, O'Meara, Powell and Garvis) where two examples of practice-based approaches are shown with kinaesthetic learning with children aged three years and four years. The chapter is written from key insights of experienced teachers and educators in the field within a Reggio Emilia approach. Within the case studies, children are given opportunities to express their learning and understanding in multiple ways.

Chapter 5 by Wu and Goff, explores how kinaesthetic learning of mathematics with young children can be supported. Bodily movements are discussed as part of practice orientation. The chapter also shares insights into how kinaesthetic teaching and learning of mathematics can be incorporated into contexts of play.

Watson and Delaney, in Chapter 6, engage with the use of vignettes to highlight the diversity of ways teachers can plan for movement in their classrooms with young children. Key concepts around embodied learning to assist the construction of knowledge and meaning are reflected upon.

In Chapter 7 (Chapman) a theoretical reflection is presented on the pedagogy of practice of kinaesthetic learning with young children. The relationship between kinaesthetic learning and arts knowledge is explored, with examples of research and practice to demonstrate constructs and pedagogical practices.

The book next moves to Chapter 8 (Barton and Trimble-Roles) where exploring quality children's literature from a project that supports boys' literacy learning in the early years through kinaesthetic approaches is shared. The project relies on the boys creating digital, multimodal texts. The chapter reports on a student-driven and collaborative learning process to support stronger notions of learning and knowledge growth.

Chapter 9 (Fanshawe, Mandarakas, Cain, Turner, White, Oddoux, Angelier and Havgaard) is a conceptual chapter that explores how careful design of play-based experiences can impact children's learning. The toy LEGO is used to support a bridge between Early Childhood Education and formal school settings.

In Chapter 10 (Kangas, Ukkonen-Mikkola and Harju-Luukkainen), the authors engage with a case study to demonstrate how teachers in Early Childhood Education and Care conceptualise and use kinaesthetic learning through embodiment guidance and scaffolding. A visual image is presented of the findings to show core concepts of kinaesthetic, active and embodied learning.

In the final chapter of the book (Chapter 11, Conclusion), key concepts are shared on kinaesthetic overall across the literature and key messages highlighted. The messages are relevant for teachers, parents, policymakers and those wanting to support better integration of kinaesthetic learning into the lives of young children. We hope that this book becomes a starting point for further discussions on the importance of kinaesthetic learning in learning and development and prompts further research within the area to support young children learning as well as teacher knowledge and development about how to support kinaesthetic learning.

References

Dalcroze Australia (n.d.). Dalcroze. www.dalcroze.org.au/dalcroze-eurythmics

Deans, J. (2016). Thinking, feeling and relating: Young children learning through dance. *Australasian Journal of Early Childhood, 41*(3), 46–57.

Deans, J., Meiners, J., & Young, S. (2012). Dance: Art embodied. In C. Sinclair, N. Jeanneret & J. O'Toole (Eds.), *Education in the Arts* (2nd ed., pp. 132–144). Oxford, UK: Oxford University Press.

Harris, S.J., & Livesey, D, J. (1992). Improving handwriting through kinaesthetic sensitivity practice. *Australian Occupational Therapy, 39*(1), 23–27.

Hudson, K.N., Ballou, H.W., & Willoughby, M.T. (2020). Short report: Improving motor competence skills in early childhood has corollary benefits for executive function and numeracy skills. *Developmental Science, 24*(4). doi: 10.1111/desc.13071

Richards, J.C., & Rodgers, T.S. (2001). *Approaches and methods in language teaching*. New York: Cambridge University Press.

Samsudin, M., Bakar, K. and Noor, N. (2019). The benefits of music and movement in early mathematics. *Creative Education*, 10, 3071–3081. doi: 10.4236/ce.2019.1012231

Sühendan, E. (2013). Using total physical response method in early childhood foreign language teaching environments. *Procedia- Social and Behavioural Sciences, 93*, 1766–1768.

Sutapa, P., & Suharjana, S. (2019). Improving gross motor skills by gross kinesthetic- and contemporary-based physical activity in early childhood. *Jurnal Cakrawala Pendidikan, 38*(3), 540–551.

Tranquillo, J. (2008, June). Kinesthetic learning in the classroom. In *2008 Annual Conference & Exposition* (pp. 13–829).

United Nations Educational, Scientific and Cultural Organization. (n.d.). *Early childhood care and education*. Retrieved from: www.unesco.org/en/education/early-childhood

Wright, S. (Ed.). (2003). *Children, meaning-making and the arts*. Frenchs Forest, NSW: Prentice Hall.

Kinaesthetic learning

A systematic review in Early Childhood Education contexts

Susanne Garvis,
Georgina Barton and Anh Hai Le

Introduction

Early Childhood Education and Care is a growing field around the world as countries look to support young children's learning and development. A key focus has been on early prevention to support children in positive learning trajectories (Anderson et al., 2003). In this chapter, we explore the role of kinaesthetic learning with young children. We are particularly interested to create a shared understanding across the research literature of key themes for children aged birth to five years, as well as gaps in current research. Given the importance of kinaesthetic learning to support positive learning and development, it is important to also share research understandings to build knowledge and understanding within Early Childhood Education and Care.

Focus of study

Based on an initial search of the literature, it appeared there were limited reviews of kinaesthetic learning in Early Childhood Education. To help fill this void, we undertook a systematic review engaging with the PRISMA approach. The review of literature would allow us to identify key themes across the literature, as well as identify gaps to identify needs for future research within Early Childhood Education.

DOI: 10.4324/9781003268772-2

Methods

Selection of articles

A systematic search was performed to identify all literature pertaining to kinaesthetic learning (KL) in Early Childhood contexts. To guide this research, a brief scoping review and evaluation of key research on kinaesthetic learning in various contexts were conducted to identify common terminology and implement a more in-depth search. The Preferred Reporting Items for Systematic Reviews and Meta-Analyses (PRISMA) recommendations were adhered to, as described by Nagendrababu et al. (2019). The primary search strategy included electronic searches in A+ Education (via Informit), Education database (via ProQuest), ERIC (via ProQuest), SPORTDiscus with Full Text (via EBSCOhost), PsycINFO (via Ovid) and Scopus. This review included only studies published from 2012 through 2022. This inclusion timeframe was selected to reflect the most recent, accurate, and extensive (long-standing) evidence-based peer-reviewed studies.

Identification of articles

The researchers used the advanced search function and entered the search terms such as "kinaesthetic learning" and other related concepts such as "hands-on learning", "learning through play", "physical play", "movement and learning" and the Boolean operator "OR" was used to combine the multiple search terms to obtain relevant results relating to Early Childhood contexts. The abstracts and titles of all the retrieved articles were independently reviewed for relevance. If deemed relevant and eligible, the full text was retrieved for a full review. Each eligible article's reference list was also reviewed for other articles with similar themes to improve the results of the search. The eligible papers from these searches were then read and screened using the inclusion and exclusion criteria established for this systematic review, as illustrated in Table 2.1.

This study's inclusion and exclusion criteria set the boundaries and scope for the scholarly publications that were included in the final review. These criteria were determined after the establishment and refinement of the research topic and the objectives. A variety of factors were considered

Table 2.1 Inclusion and exclusion criteria

Inclusion Criteria	Exclusion Criteria
Addressed KL in an Early Childhood setting	Addressed KL in other settings than Early Childhood
Published from 2012 through 2022	Published before 2012
Written in English	Non-English publication
Peer-reviewed journal	Not a peer-reviewed journal
Published study	Unpublished study (e.g., proposal and ongoing project)
Full-text access	No access to full-text version

in formulating the eligibility criteria to define a practical scope of analysis, enhance the study's focus and ensure the inclusion of only recent articles.

Data extraction and synthesis

The data were extracted using Microsoft Word tables and undertaken with the appropriate synthesis in mind. Microsoft Word, an application by an American multinational technology, was chosen because it allowed the researcher to create tables for the easy extraction and synthesis of the data. To chart the data from the extracted studies, the researcher created a descriptive summary of the results that addressed the objectives and research questions previously stated in the introductory section of this review. A draft of the charting template was developed to allow efficient data coding. The charting form was left open to allow editing and additional unforeseen data during the analysis, which allowed the process to be iterative. The key items on the charting form included the author, year of publication, age range, types of kinaesthetic learning (i.e., activity type), benefits of kinaesthetic learning including developmental impacts (i.e., social and emotional, language/communication, movement/physical development, and cognitive-learning, thinking, problem-solving).

A thematic analysis protocol was used in the synthesis of data recorded on the charting form after data gathering/extraction. Thematic synthesis, as described by Ryan et al. (2018), provides a range of established techniques and methods for the identification and development of analytical themes for the purpose of secondary data synthesis. This method was adopted in this review for three reasons. First, the process of synthesis provides transparency, and the outcomes are easily accessible (Ryan et al., 2018). Second, thematic synthesis is also used for the synthesis of both quantitative and qualitative data. Third, this method was suited to the objectives of the present study, as it aimed to aggregate evidence and highlight patterns within the data. This process was conducted in three stages, with all steps applied to all studies, including both qualitative and quantitative analyses. The first stage involved coding (identification of text or other data items), as described on the charting form. Each article that was identified after the inclusion and exclusion criteria was read twice to ensure that every item was coded. The second phase involved analysing the similarities between the codes related to kinaesthetic learning in Early Childhood Education, and these were categorised as "descriptive themes" and "descriptive patterns" across the included studies. These descriptive patterns and themes are presented subsequently to facilitate comparisons within and between studies for reporting and discussion. The final step involved the establishment of analytic themes to allow the researcher to synthesise the findings across studies and interpret their meanings.

Results

Search results

The searches revealed 546 articles from the databases, of which 55 were duplicates, thereby reducing the number of articles to 491. After reviewing their titles and abstracts, 245 articles were excluded because they did not meet the inclusion criteria regarding document type, language, or focus of the study. The findings reported in those studies did not satisfy the objectives of this study in terms of reporting kinaesthetic learning in Early Childhood contexts, leaving 245 full-text articles being assessed for eligibility. After full-text reviews, 222 additional studies were excluded due to inclusive findings about kinaesthetic learning (i.e., no description of learning outcomes regarding developmental impacts), not being conducted in Early Childhood contexts, and not empirical studies but reviews of perspectives. The complete process resulted in 23 articles for qualitative analysis.

Results of the thematic analysis

The thematic analysis results indicated that kinaesthetic learning has posi-tive impacts on different areas of a child's development including cognitive, social and emotional, speech and language, fine motor and gross motor skill development. Table 2.2 summarises key studies illuminating the develop-mental impacts of different types of kinaesthetic learning (i.e., types of play activities).

Discussion

Across the research literature, key themes emerge around the age of chil-dren, types of kinaesthetic learning, developmental impacts and participants in the research. Each theme will be discussed below.

Age of children

The majority of articles reviewed show that older children (3–5 years) was the most common age range with children participating from either kindergarten or preschool. A small number of studies did have children aged under 3, however this was mainly with children aged 1–2 years. This may have been because of age requirements for starting the Early Childhood service (for example in Sweden children can start at 1 year of age but not before). The research profiling of age also is consistent with the current gaps of research with children aged under 3 around the world. Early childhood Education research appears to have children aged 3 years and above who are verbal, with many countries having universal access from 3 years of age. However, there is a strong need in the research litera-ture for research with children aged under 3 years, especially in countries where attendance at Early Childhood services can start from 6 weeks of age (as in Australia).

Types of kinaesthetic activities

The majority of activities involved an element of play. This consisted of either free play, parent-child play interactions, guided play, multi-vocal

Table 2.2 Summary of the key findings from the included studies

#	Age grouping	Types of kinaesthetic learning	Developmental impacts	Author(s)/Date
1	kindergarten	building blocks	mathematical learning	Kinzer et al. (2016)
2	kindergarten	card and board games	mathematical learning	Vogt et al. (2018)
3	preschool	draw-and-tell	expressing preferences	Wiseman et al. (2018)
4	preschool	free play	emotional and social functioning	Veiga et al. (2016)
5	preschool	free play	language	Dominguez et al. (2018)
6	preschool	free play & structured activities	motor skills	Tortella et al. (2016)
7	kindergarten	guided play	literacy	Cavanaugh et al. (2017)
8	preschool	guided play	literacy	Strauss & Bipath (2020)
9	kindergarten	guided pretend play	problem-solving	Hollenstein et al. (2022)
10	early childhood	make-believe play	social and academic competence	Germeroth et al. (2019)
11	preschool	multimodal and multi-vocal play	language	Countryman & Gabriel (2014)
12	kindergarten	outdoor activities	wellbeing	Bjørgen (2015)
13	early childhood (0–3)	parent-child play interactions	cognitive and socio-emotional	Amodia-Bidakowska et al. (2020)
14	preschool	parent-child play interactions	language and literacy	Stockall & Dennis (2013)
15	preschool	patterning	mathematical learning	Colliver (2018)

(continued)

Table 2.2 Cont.

#	Age grouping	Types of kinaesthetic learning	Developmental impacts	Author(s)/Date
16	early childhood (3–4)	physical activity	movement Skills	Ali et al. (2021)
17	early childhood (4 years old)	problem-solving activities	literacy and numeracy	Colliver & Arguel (2018)
18	preschool	science outdoors	early science	Kos et al. (2015)
19	preschool	social play (fantasy, role, exercise or rough-and-tumble)	social competence	Veiga et al. (2017)
20	kindergarten	story telling-based and play-based	social competence	Aksoy & Baran (2020)
21	preschool	Successful Kinaesthetic Instruction for Pre-schoolers (SKIP)	motor skill	Mulvey et al. (2020)
22	early childhood (2 years old)	tool-mediated activities	social competence	Kultti & Pramling (2015)
23	early childhood (0–4)	web-based games	literacy	Schmitt et al. (2018)

play, pretend play, make-believe play and social play. This also suggests that there is strong acknowledgement in the research of the importance of play to support kinaesthetic learning activities. It could be that play allows children to create and move in their own space to support their own individual learning. While play has an element of flexibility, other activities had more structure. This included activities such as tool-mediated activities, web-based games, draw-and-tell and building blocks. Tools are provided to support the child in movement and activity. The tool is usually linked to a specific content area to support. In one paper, direct instruction was identified to support kinaesthetic learning with preschool-age children. It was surprising that little focus was given to direct instruction in the research literature. However, it may be a focus of Early Childhood curricula around the world to concentrate on "free play" or agency for young children. However, it does also show a gap in that there is limited research around intentional teaching/direct instruction with kinaesthetic learning in Early Childhood however a number of Early Years curricula around the world advocate for a balance between intentional teaching and play. The lack of focus may also be explained by different views of children and agency regarding varying paradigms in Early Childhood Education that may be more dominant in some countries or regions than others.

Developmental impacts

A wide range of developmental areas was reflected across the review of research literature including language/literacy, mathematics, science, social and emotional wellbeing and motor skills. The majority of areas were around literacy/language and social and emotional wellbeing. This could be because of the type of activity (most likely linked to elements of play) and the current time snap of child development. One research paper was linked to science, again showing the growing importance of science education in Early Years and recent movements around the world to include science education in Early Years curricula.

Certain specific content areas, however, were missing, such as arts, coding or technology. In recent years, these activities have been included in a number of Early Years curricula around the world to support young children's learning and development. In particular, it was surprising to see a limited focus on arts and kinaesthetic activities, especially given certain activities such as dance and movement within the arts. One possibility may be that certain search terms did not allow these papers to become recognised, or alternatively, there is a current lack of research in Early Childhood Education between kinaesthetic movement and these content areas.

Participants

While the majority of participants were children, in a small number of papers, parent-child interaction emerged. This is important to acknowledge that within Early Childhood Education and Care, there are three actors – child, teacher and parent – who work together. Parent research is starting to be an emerging field within Early Childhood Education research as the importance of parental involvement is recognised for children's learning. There is also a greater acknowledgement that parents are the "first educator" of children and become partners in the learning process. More research is needed around the importance of parental involvement, especially with the youngest of children in Early Childhood services.

Conclusion

The intention of this chapter was to review current research literature associated with kinaesthetic learning and Early Childhood Education to provide a snapshot of current themes to support understandings. What emerged from the papers selected was that the majority of participants were aged over 3 and engaged in play activities that were linked to language/literacy or social and emotional wellbeing. The activities were usually unstructured and allowed children to engage in their own kinaesthetic learning. Across the themes also emerged gaps, such as research with the youngest of children, a focus on content areas that may appear in Early Years curricula (such as arts, technology and coding) and the role of parents in Early Childhood Education research. What is clear, however, is that kinaesthetic learning in Early Childhood Education is a growing field that is building in reputation and empirical evidence. We hope that as more evidence develops in the research, kinaesthetic learning can be supported across all Early Years curricula around the world to support young children's learning and development.

References

Aksoy, P., & Baran, G. (2020). The effect of story telling-based and play-based social skills training on social skills of kindergarten children: An experimental study. *Egitim ve Bilim*, *45*(204), 157–183.

Ali, A., McLachlan, C., Mugridge, O., McLaughlin, T., Conlon, C., & Clarke, L. (2021). The effect of a 10-week physical activity programme on fundamental movement skills in 3–4-year-old children within early childhood education centres. *Children*, *8*(6), 440.

Amodia-Bidakowska, A., Laverty, C., & Ramchandani, P. G. (2020). Father-child play: A systematic review of its frequency, characteristics and potential impact on children's development. *Developmental Review*, *57*, 100924.

Anderson, L. M., Shinn, C., Fullilove, M. T., Scrimshaw, S. C., Fielding, J. E., Normand, J., ... & Task Force on Community Preventive Services. (2003). The effectiveness of early childhood development programs: A systematic review. *American Journal of Preventive Medicine*, *24*(3), 32–46.

Bjørgen, K. (2015). Children's well-being and involvement in physically active outdoors play in a Norwegian kindergarten: Playful sharing of physical experiences. *Child Care in Practice*, *21*(4), 305–323.

Cavanaugh, D. M., Clemence, K. J., Teale, M. M., Rule, A. C., & Montgomery, S. E. (2017). Kindergarten scores, storytelling, executive function, and motivation improved through literacy-rich guided play. *Early Childhood Education Journal*, *45*(6), 831–843.

Colliver, Y. (2018). Fostering young children's interest in numeracy through demonstration of its value: the Footsteps Study. *Mathematics Education Research Journal*, *30*(4), 407–428.

Colliver, Y., & Arguel, A. (2018). Following in our footsteps: How adult demonstrations of literacy and numeracy can influence children's spontaneous play and improve learning outcomes. *Early Child Development and Care*, *188*(8), 1093–1108.

Countryman, J., & Gabriel, M. A. (2014). Recess as a site for language play. *Language and Literacy*, *16*(3), 4–26.

Dominguez, S., & Trawick-Smith, J. (2018). A qualitative study of the play of dual language learners in an English-speaking preschool. *Early Childhood Education Journal*, *46*(6), 577–586.

Germeroth, C., Bodrova, E., Day-Hess, C., Barker, J., Sarama, J., Clements, D. H., & Layzer, C. (2019). Play it high, play it low: Examining the reliability and validity of a new observation tool to measure children's make-believe play. *American Journal of Play*, *11*(2), 183–221.

Hollenstein, L., Thurnheer, S., & Vogt, F. (2022). Problem solving and digital transformation: Acquiring skills through pretend play in kindergarten. *Education Sciences*, *12*(2), 92.

Kinzer, C., Gerhardt, K., & Coca, N. (2016). Building a case for blocks as kinder-garten mathematics learning tools. *Early Childhood Education Journal, 44*(4), 389–402.

Kos, M., Šuperger, B., & Jerman, J. (2015). Early science outdoors: Learning about trees in the preschool period. *Problems of Education in the 21st Century, 64*, 24.

Kultti, A., & Pramling, N. (2015). Bring your own toy: Socialisation of two-year-olds through tool-mediated activities in an Australian early childhood education context. *Early Childhood Education Journal, 43*(5), 367–376.

Mulvey, K. L., Miedema, S. T., Stribing, A., Gilbert, E., & Brian, A. (2020). Skiping together: A motor competence intervention promotes gender-integrated friendships for young children. *Sex Roles, 82*(9), 550–557.

Nagendrababu, V., Duncan, H. F., Tsesis, I., Sathorn, C., Pulikkotil, S. J., Dharmarajan, L., & Dummer, P. M. H. (2019). Preferred reporting items for systematic reviews and meta-analyses for abstracts: Best practice for reporting abstracts of systematic reviews in Endodontology. *International Endodontic Journal, 52*(8), 1096–1107.

Ryan, C., Hesselgreaves, H., Wu, O., Paul, J., Dixon-Hughes, J., & Moss, J. G. (2018). Protocol for a systematic review and thematic synthesis of patient experiences of central venous access devices in anti-cancer treatment. *Systematic Reviews, 7*(1), 1–7.

Schmitt, K. L., Hurwitz, L. B., Duel, L. S., & Linebarger, D. L. N. (2018). Learning through play: The impact of web-based games on early literacy development. *Computers in Human Behavior, 81*, 378–389.

Stockall, N., & Dennis, L. (2013). Fathers' role in play: Enhancing early language and literacy of children with developmental delays. *Early Childhood Education Journal, 41*(4), 299–306.

Strauss, A. M., & Bipath, K. (2020). Expanding vocabulary and sight word growth through guided play in a pre-primary classroom. *South African Journal of Childhood Education, 10*(1), 1–9.

Tortella, P., Haga, M., Loras, H., Sigmundsson, H., & Fumagalli, G. (2016). Motor skill development in Italian pre-school children induced by structured activities in a specific playground. *PloS One, 11*(7), e0160244.

Veiga, G., De Leng, W., Cachucho, R., Ketelaar, L., Kok, J. N., Knobbe, A., ... & Rieffe, C. (2017). Social competence at the playground: Preschoolers during recess. *Infant and Child Development, 26*(1), e1957.

Veiga, G., Neto, C., & Rieffe, C. (2016). Preschoolers' free play: Connections with emotional and social functioning. *International Journal of Emotional Education, 8*, 48–62.

Vogt, F., Hauser, B., Stebler, R., Rechsteiner, K., & Urech, C. (2018). Learning through play–pedagogy and learning outcomes in early childhood mathematics. *European Early Childhood Education Research Journal, 26*(4), 589–603.

Wiseman, N., Rossmann, C., Lee, J., & Harris, N. (2018). "It's like you are in the jungle": Using the draw-and-tell method to explore preschool children's play preferences and factors that shape their active play. *Health Promotion Journal of Australia, 30*, 85–94.

Learning-by-doing

A self-narrative approach to children's experiential learning

Tina Yngvesson and
Susanne Garvis

Introduction

'Learning-by-doing' is a term often associated with learning from experience. In this chapter, we explore concepts of 'learning-by-doing' in two
different contexts, Sweden and Australia, within Early Childhood Education
and Care. We are particularly interested in children's motivators for experiential learning and how they can be seen within children's everyday activities. We engage in this type of self-narrative case study (Kitchen, 2009)
to also understand and unpack our understandings of learning to better
explore opportunities to support, connect and extend young children's
learning.

We align with the approaches of John Dewey who believed that young
children should have socially engaging learning experiences that are developmentally appropriate (Dewey, 1938). As such, Dewey, considered education to be a "process of living and not a preparation for future living"
(Flinders & Thornton, 2013, p. 35; Gutek, 2014). This also means that children and their learning should be seen as unique and individualist, where
they are busy constructing their own knowledge and personal meaning,
rather than teacher-directed activities (Schiro, 2013). Rather, learning occurs
when children are doing – within a concept of learning-by-doing where
problem-solving and knowledge construction is created through hands-on

DOI: 10.4324/9781003268772-3

approaches (Williams, 2017). Unfortunately, this approach to learning, especially with young children may not be understood and recognised for the actual benefit to children's individual learning and development.

In this chapter, we draw on two different countries (Sweden and Australia) to also show similarities in young children's learning and the importance of providing space for learning-by-doing. We also draw on these countries as they are based in different parts of the world and have different approaches to Early Childhood Education for young children. We engage specifically with narrative research within the case studies that align with pragmatic approaches. Narrative research is often inspired by a view of human experience that is based on John Dewey's pragmatic philosophy (Clandinin, 2006). This chapter, allows human experience to be explored through the telling and retelling of children's learning-by-doing.

Context of study

Swedish Early Childhood Education

Children in Sweden are commonly enrolled at preschool from the age of 12–24 months and may attend between the hours of 6 am and 6 pm all year, with the exception of four weeks during the summer. Well known for its generous family policy, Sweden aims to support the reconciliation of work and family life (Duvander, 2008; Haas, 1996) and the well-being of children. Thus, democratic values such as civil rights, equality, equity and solidarity are central components of the Swedish welfare model and during the last century, Sweden has concretised its social democratic model in an effort to develop a more equal society regarding social security systems and equal opportunities for men and women (Duvander, 2008; Wells & Bergnehr, 2014). Hence, the introduction of reforms such as parental leave, child allowance as well as access to preschool for all children have resulted in children becoming the responsibility of not only the family but also society (Broström, Einarsdottir & Pramling Samuelsson, 2018), on par with compulsory school education.

The Swedish preschool is governed by 1) the Education Act, which regulates children's rights and obligations from an educational perspective and 2) the Curriculum for Preschool, Lpfö18, which describes the preschool's values, pedagogical content, and responsibilities of preschool teachers and the principals (Swedish National Agency for Education, 2018). The primary task of the preschool is defined as one ensuring the overall healthy development of every child, in terms of intellectual, social and developmental needs (Swedish National Agency for Education, 2018).

The Swedish preschool takes a holistic view of the child and the national approach to learning is that every child should be given a forum to learn according to his or her own preconditions. In the Curriculum for Preschool, Lpfö 18 (Swedish National Agency for Education) it is stated in the goals of section 2.2, *Care, development and learning*, that "Education in the preschool should take its starting point in the curriculum and in children's needs, experiences and what they show an interest in. The flow of children's thoughts and ideas should be utilised to create diversity in learning" (p. 14). Under the specific aims of preschool education, kinaesthetic learning can be interpreted as expressed under several of the curriculum's guidelines. These are that the preschool teacher is responsible for providing the child with:

- an ability to create and an ability to express and communicate occurrences, thoughts and experiences in different forms of expression such as image, form, drama, movement, singing, music and dance;
- an interest in stories, pictures and texts in different media, both digital and other, and their ability to use, interpret, question and discuss them;
- an ability to use mathematics to investigate, reflect on and try out different solutions to problems raised by themselves and others;
- an understanding of space, time and form, and the basic properties of sets, patterns, quantities, order, numbers, measurement and change, and to reason mathematically about this;
- being challenged and stimulated in her or his development of language and communication, as well as mathematics, science and technology, and
- being able to use digital tools in a way that stimulates development and learning (pp. 15–16).

By including these guidelines in the curriculum, the national recognition of the importance of blending various ways of learning to promote development is made visible. The curriculum aims to engage the child in cognitive, motor, and sensory development in all subject fields, with the overarching intention to provide the child with skills to support lifelong learning.

Australian Early Childhood Education

Australian Early Childhood Education accommodates children aged birth to five years. Children can be located in long day care centres (birth to five year all-day programmes), kindergartens (three to five-year-old children and usually run 9am to 3pm) family day care, (birth to five years all-day programmes) private early learning centres (three to five-year-olds and usually run 9am to 3pm) and outside school hours care (before school care and after school care).

In Australia, there is the National Quality Framework (ACECQA, n.d.) that provides a national approach to regulation, quality improvement and assessment of the Early Childhood Education sector. The National Quality Framework consists of a national learning framework for children to ensure quality learning and development. The intention is that early learning services base their programming on an approved learning framework to support every child. While kinaesthetic learning is mentioned within *Belonging, Being and Becoming: Early Years Learning Framework for Australia* (DEEWR, 2009) movement is mentioned with Outcome 3 and Outcome 5.

> Outcome 3 Children's learning and physical development is evident through their movement patterns from physical dependence and reflex actions at birth, to the integration of sensory, motor and cognitive systems for organised, controlled physical activity for both purpose and enjoyment.
>
> (p. 33)

> Outcome 5 Literacy is the capacity, confidence and disposition to use language in all its forms. Literacy incorporates a range of modes of communication including music, movement, dance, storytelling, visual arts, media and drama, as well as talking, listening, viewing, reading and writing.
>
> (p. 41)

This suggests that there is recognition of the importance of movement with young children to support learning and development. This includes sensory, motor, and cognitive, as well as key learning areas such as literacy. The intention is Early Years teachers plan for children's movement to work towards and support children's learning for Outcome 3 and Outcome 5.

Focus of study

In this study, we draw upon two self-narratives as case studies to unpack examples of children's experiential learning in Sweden and Australia. The two self-narratives are shared by the authors who are parents, teachers and researchers who have "an authority of experience" (Munby & Russell, 1994) and "craft knowledge" of education (Grimmett, 1995). The authors engage in these three identities to share their experiences across the different educational systems and draw upon opportunities for children's intrinsic and extrinsic motivation. Through unpacking the stories, similarities can be made across the countries as well as emerging differences.

Methods

In this chapter, a narrative self-study was employed that consisted of a case study in Sweden and a case study in Australia. Narrative self-studies are an important tool for developing and sharing hidden meanings within teaching and teaching practice, including the complexity of relationships. As Kitchen (2009, p. 38) states:

> Self-study is the noun because the focus of narrative self-study is the improvement of practice by reflecting on oneself and one's practices as a teacher educator. Narrative, the adjective, refers to the use of specific narrative inquiry methods to study ourselves and our practices in order to improve practice.

Through this narrative approach, we were able to tell and retell our own stories within our own professional practices (Kitchen, 2009), allowing us to develop critical understandings of experiential learning. Through the sharing of our narratives we also engaged in a better understanding of our personal practical knowledge as teachers (Clandinin & Connelly, 2004). The creation of the text "looks backward and forward, looks inward and outward, and situates the experience within place" (Clandinin & Connelly, 2000, p. 14). Through such reflecting, we were able to look beyond surface-level understandings of experience by critiquing inherent meanings within teaching and teaching practices. The approach also allowed us to recreate and reimagine extrinsic learning in relation to motivation.

In each section, we both begin by reflecting on our experiences as a parent, before pivoting to reflections as a teacher and then moving to the final stage of reflections as a researcher. We move from the present back in time throughout the reflections. Within each case study we also include photos to show examples.

Results

Case 1: Australia

My child entered the Australian Early Childhood system in August 2020 during COVID, aged 2 years and 10 months. The centre in Victoria was familiar with the Victorian Early Years Learning and Development Framework (Victorian Department of Education and Training, 2016), a framework to support young children's learning and development. At the heart of the framework was the acknowledgement of the ecological systems model (p. 5) where the child was placed in the centre of the model and acknowledged as being shaped by family, culture and experience. As such, this also meant that Early Years services were an important contributor in the child's learning by providing a wide range of experiences that enhanced the child's learning and development.

My daughter began with a range of choice through the day of activities with the ability to move to activities set up inside (such as play centres of book corner, dress ups, home corner, puzzles) or outside (climbing frames, balls, sand pit, painting). The activities would change over time. Children when venturing outside were encouraged to take off their shoes to also experience outside textures such as cement, sand and grass. Sometimes throughout the day, the children would come together (children were aged 1 to 5 years of age) or at other times they could choose their own friends to play with. On some days, a kindergarten programme operated for 4-year-old children (15 hours a week).

My daughter was immediately drawn to having play activities across the day that also encouraged experiential learning. One example was how to create a unicorn mask. My daughter was obsessed with unicorns and wanted to create a specific mask so she could become one. She worked with the teachers on a plan of what she needed and how she would construct the unicorn. Throughout the experience, she experimented with different materials to stand up the face mask, before settling on straws. She also realised that the straw needed to be connected to the paper, and again experimented with glue and other types of tape before settling on masking tape. My daughter also realised that colour was needed for the mask, and in particular, bright colours to represent the unicorn.

This type of learning allowed my daughter to engage in her own problem-solving and engage in kinaesthetic learning through manipulating different materials. After the product was created through an experimental process, she engaged in imaginary play with the masks for extended periods of time.

I now jump back in time to when I was a teacher with young children in their first years of schooling. I remember a particular event where we asked children to identify a problem and then asked them to engage in a plan to help solve the problem (problem-based learning). We began by initially going on a walk around the school to explore areas the children thought needed improvement. Straight away, having more trees in the school for shade and to support animals became a priority area for the children. The children also liked to undertake leaf paintings and realised that more trees would mean more leaves to use for these unique paintings. We began to write on large pieces of paper what would solve the problem and bringing in more trees immediately came as a solution. We then brainstormed on how this might happen. Over time and working with the community, the children realised that by talking with the local councillor, they were able to have 20 trees delivered that could be planted at the school.

Again over a Friday, we planted 20 trees in a designated area around the school (after agreement from the principal and school gardener) and each child was given a tree to look after. Each day the tree would have to be inspected, watered and fertilised as necessary. Over a period of 6 months, the children also developed an observation diary to draw pictures of the trees as they developed and also to document the different seasons and how this impacted the growth of the trees.

The experiential learning experience of allowing children to solve an issue they faced at the school. It showed they were able to develop a number of problem-solving skills to extend their own knowledge and understanding of science, environmental sustainability, governance, numeracy and literacy. Children regularly engaged in kinaesthetic activities throughout the learning process such as digging holes for the trees and regularly drawing and writing what they were seeing about the tree as it developed. The children were able to engage in movement activities within the learning to support their understanding of development cycles within nature as well as improve their own skills associated with gross and fine motor movement.

I now stay in the past but shift my identity to a researcher and teacher educator. I reflect on a teaching activity 10 years ago to promote kinaesthetic learning with Early Childhood teacher education pre-service teachers. As part of an Early Childhood programme, pre-service teachers develop knowledge and skills of children aged birth to five years. While pre-service teachers are generally comfortable working with children who are verbal, children who are pre-verbal may create some anxiety. In Australia, children can start Early Childhood services before one year of age. This was raised by pre-service teachers as a particular area of need. To help develop skills, I decided to replicate a 'real world' scenario of looking after infants by hiring 'computer babies' that are programmed to cry, sleep, wake, and babble. Sometimes such 'computer babies' are used within high schools to experience teenage parenthood. In this instance, I wanted the pre-service teachers to also experience the baby, but also the possibility of babies, with the expectation that an educator could possibly look after four babies at once with current ratio requirements in Early Childhood settings.

The activity occurred over a couple of days, where plenty of role-playing allowed the educator to role-play by entering into character and looking after each baby. Each baby was programmed differently for their needs, meaning they would cry, sleep and need to be fed at different times. Pre-service teachers were also expected to create notes and observations of the babies at the same time and think about possible learning activities.

At the end of the activity, the pre-service teachers commented on how much they had learnt from actually having to undertake the role of being an educator for children aged under one year of age. In particular, how this was practical learning that allowed them to actually have to actively think about what they would do next and how they would support the baby in the moment. The pre-service teachers suggested that this type of learning was not possible in just lectures and workshops, with most activities being based on discussion, learning theories or answering questions. This activity allowed the pre-service teachers to be 'hands-on' and actually start to practise what they had been learning about in Early Childhood teacher education. It also made me realise how we need to have more opportunities for kinaesthetic learning in Early Childhood Education to allow mastery of experience for pre-service teachers.

Case 2: Sweden

My first experience with the Swedish preschool system was August 2013, when my firstborn son was 15 months old. He enrolled in a Montessori preschool, situated outside of Gothenburg (Swedish west coast) amidst trees and fields. Choosing Montessori was a conscious decision and one we made after interviewing several local preschools. This particular preschool had only three children per preschool teacher and the majority of staff were a fully trained preschool teachers, many of them with specific training in Montessori pedagogy. At 15 months old, my son had not yet begun to engage in play with other children and would spend quite a lot of time (according to the teachers) with building blocks. Not interested in participating with the other children, he was happy being part of the children's praxis and community on his own terms, which meant playing by himself, on the periphery. Rather than pushing him into the group, the teachers allowed for this individual development, embracing every child's unique needs and abilities, which meant he was provided space and time for investigating the world around him on his own terms.

By the time he was two years old, he had developed an interest in border crossing and would on his own initiative engineer constructions that he would then draw or paint. These were not organised pedagogical activities, rather they were child-led activities driven by intrinsic motivators stemming from his two-year-old self.

His need to assert himself through establishing something and then depicting it to somehow eternalise it became a trend in how he did this. By the time he was three, he would go into the preschool yard, collect flowers and take them back to work with them, with glue, with glitter, paper, and scissors, in order to create gardens of his own. Catching his interests, the teachers would encourage this exploration of materials in combination with the natural sciences and aesthetics, allowing him to use all his senses, from seeing and identifying the flowers to touching and picking them to dissecting them into various parts and then blending them, or parts of them, with other materials. All the while free of gloves and aprons, which was a deliberate part of the learning process; if he spilled, it made a stain on his clothes and so he learned to manage his hands carefully. The philosophy of the preschool was very much founded on the idea that 'if you cannot do it by yourself, then you are not ready', and so you must continue practicing. Through this practice, my son developed his problem-solving skills and on his own terms engaged in kinaesthetic learning exploring and investigating with different materials.

This idea that children's intrinsic motivators can act as a powerful drive and tool when learning, is an ideology that I carried with me as a few years later worked as an educator with preschool children. I recall one particular event where my colleague and I had some trouble engaging the class in mathematics. It was simple arithmetics and the children were five years old. It was hard for them to focus and albeit several of the children were keen learners, on this particular day it was a challenge to maintain their focus for any length of time. To solve this problem, we decided to take the learning outdoors. Once we ushered them all outside, we divided them into two groups of 9 (they were 18 children all in all) and asked them to 'make seven'. The first group quickly laid down, making the shape of seven lying down on the ground. The second group placed four children in one group, three children in one group, and the remaining two laid down across one another, forming a 'plus' sign. This continued and the problem-solving advanced, for each task the children would discuss and decide how to 'best do the maths'. Soon, they shifted from using only their own bodies to collecting natural artefacts, such as sticks, stones, or fallen leaves with which they would artistically design arithmetic and present the correct answers, either verbally or by demonstrating the answer with a natural artefact.

The above demonstrates a type of experiential learning experience that is very free-form and allows the child to develop their understanding through engaging both physically and intellectually (Broström, Einarsdottir & Pramling Samuelsson, 2018). Throughout these learning processes, the children regularly engaged in kinaesthetic activities with both each other and with nature, allowing them to integrate learning across borders (Gutek, 2014). Applying both gross and fine motor skills, depending on whether they were arranging their own bodies into numbers on the ground or fine strands of grass into mathematical equations, the children applied both movement, mind, and cognition to interact with one another and with nature. Whilst being beneficial for the child on many levels, this approach was also in line with the curriculum which promotes a holistic view of the child where learning and development are seen as an ecological process (Swedish Agency for Education, 2018).

Fast forward to my current role as a pre-service preschool teacher educator and aspiring researcher in Early Childhood Education, I reflect on how I collect and apply the various experiences that define my own understanding of child development. Having the ability to locate one's various body parts and identify how they move, is central in kinaesthetic learning and when children link the process of learning to physical activity, they oftentimes learn more effectively. As part of the first-semester course for the pre-service pre-school teachers, we do a series of five workshops where the students can practise various forms of rhetoric. Rather than focusing solely on visual, auditory, reading and writing-oriented learning, the course focuses on the student executing a physical activity in order to learn something. This means that the student is situated as an active participant in his or her own learning process, as opposed to being a passive listener of, for instance, a lecture). For instance, when learning about how to plan pedagogical activities with children, rather than watching a video and listening to lectures to then design a presentation on the given topic, the student will physically create an activity and present it to the other students and through that extending the engagement of learning also to the rest of the group. The pedagogical activity that they plan and execute must be within the curriculum and must clearly relate to what the curriculum states that the child is to be given the opportunity to learn. This can be mathematics, natural science, aesthetics, and so on. Typically, a student will plan an activity that allows the children to use theory hands, such as investigating the density of an object in water. Does a potato sink? Does an apple sink? Why? Why not? This enables the teacher to demonstrate with his or her hands, how various objects sink or float. The child can feel the weight of the object in the water by putting his or her hands in the water and holding the object, and discussions can ensue as to why things are the way they are.

At the end of these five workshops, the students reflect and discuss their own development and how they have developed practical tools for planning and teaching, rather than just gathering theoretical knowledge. The students can also take this repertoire of activities that they have seen and partaken in during the course and apply it in the field when they do their work placements. According to the collective discussions with the students at the end of the course, this increases their confidence when planning and executing pedagogical activities and also allows them to further explore the ways in which we kinaesthetically learn with children.

Key messages

When we reflect on the two self-studies, there are key messages we can reflect upon regarding kinaesthetic learning and young children. The first reflection is that children are keen to learn and express themselves in kinaesthetic ways. While the two children lived on different sides of the world (Sweden and Australia), we can point out that both enjoyed the construction of their own knowledge through engagement in activities. The approach in both countries allowed children to build their own knowledge and understanding through learning-by-doing, highlighting the learning theories advocated by Dewey. The approach was more similar and provided opportunities for the children to succeed. From the examples, it is evident that each child enjoyed the challenge of the activity (problem-solving) and wanted to extend their own knowledge in a continuous cycle. The teacher and educator were able to follow the lead of the child.

It is important that teachers and educators engaging with young children understand the importance of learning-by-doing and recognise that children develop at their individual rates when they are ready. Teachers and educators can develop understanding of children's learning in Early Childhood teacher education and we advocate for a range of learning theories to be incorporated, especially the works of Dewey and ideas around progressive education. Some modern interpretations of his work have been noted, such as responsive classroom approaches and philosophy with children (Williams, 2017). We suggest that by returning to ideas of how children learn, all children can be supported in their learning and development.

As part of the incorporation of learning-by-doing into teacher education, we also suggest a greater focus on allowing pre-service teachers to experience learning-by-doing in workshop activities. In the examples given in the two case studies, both authors provided activities that allowed pre-service teachers opportunities to engage in their own learning-by-doing. Rather than learning at the university being passive in how to become an Early Childhood teacher, we suggest that the approach could also be applied to new ways of activities within Early Childhood teacher education to support not only the learning of pre-service teachers but also provide them with opportunities to reflect on their own learning and development in relation to learning-by-doing. Through such self-reflection possibilities, greater understanding of learning and supporting learning can be achieved and developed for all young children.

Another key message is the need for more research around young children and kinaesthetic learning with examples of practice. Across the literature, while theories around learning are numerous, examples of practice in relation to theories are not. We suggest that by teachers and educators sharing practices and aligning with learning theories, we can build and develop stronger understandings across the Early Childhood profession of learning and child development. The knowledge sharing of practice also becomes a form of professional learning, allowing the Early Childhood profession to renew and refresh around children's learning and development.

Our final message is about the importance of taking the first step in sharing small case studies. While our studies do not have the generalisability of other studies, we are able to share a snapshot in time of learning-by-doing. The key is not to make groundbreaking research, but rather to create small steps for change leading to possible tipping points over time. These two case studies, in different countries, allow us to start to reflect, question, and rethink possibilities for learning with young children.

Conclusion

In this chapter, we have provided examples from two different countries of learning-by-doing with young children and in teacher education. The focus was to document children's learning and show the importance of kinaesthetic learning in Early Childhood Education. We have implemented a narrative self-study case study approach to share small stories of practice. We hope that through such retellings of stories, we can develop and share pedagogical practices that support the learning and development of all young children.

References

Australian Children's Education and Care Quality Authority (ACECQA). (n.d.) National Quality Framework. www.acecqa.gov.au/national-quality-framework

Broström, S., Einarsdottir, J. and Pramling Samuelsson, I. (2018). The nordic perspective on early childhood education and care. In M. Fleer & B. van Oers (Eds.), *International handbook of early childhood education*. 1st ed. 2018. [Online]. Dordrecht: Springer Netherlands (pp. 867–888).

Clandinin, D. J. (2006). Narrative inquiry: A methodology for studying lived experience. *Research Studies in Music Education, 27*, 44–4.

Clandinin, D. J., & Connelly, F. M. (2000). *Narrative inquiry: Experience and story in qualitative research*. San Francisco: Jossey-Bass Inc.

Clandinin, D. J., & Connelly, F. M. (2004). Knowledge, narrative and self-study. In J. J. Loughran, M. L. Hamilton, V. K. LaBoskey, & T. Russell (Eds.), *International handbook of self-study of teaching and teacher education practices* (pp. 575–600). Dordrecht: Kluwer Academic.

Department of Education Employment and Workplace Relations (DEEWR). (2009). Belonging, being and becoming: The early years learning framework for australia. Canberra, Australia: Australian Government Department of Education, Employment and Workplace Relations. Retrieved from www.acecqa.gov.au/sites/default/files/2018-02/belonging_being_and_becoming_the_early_years_learning_framework_for_australia.pdf

Dewey, J. (1938). *Experience and education*. New York: Macmillan.

Duvander, A.-Z. (2008). Family policy in Sweden: An overview. *Social Insurance Report, 15*, 1–18.

Flinders, D., & Thornton, S. (2013). *The curriculum studies reader*. (4th Ed.). New York: Routledge.

Grimmett, P. P. (1995). Reconceptualizing teacher education: Preparing teachers for revitalized schools. In M. F. Wideen & P. P. Grimmett (Eds.), *Changing times in teacher education* (pp. 202–224). London: Falmer.

Gutek, G. (2014). *Philosophical, ideological, and theoretical perspectives on education*. (2nd Ed.). Pearson.

Haas, L. (1996). Family policy in Sweden. *Journal of Family and Economic Issues, 17*, 47–92.

Kitchen, J. (2009). Passages: Improving teacher education through narrative self-study. In L. Fitzgerald, M. Heston, & D. Tidwell (Eds.), *Methods for self-study of practice* (pp. 35–51). Dordrecht: Springer.

Munby, H., & Russell, T. (1994). The authority of experience in learning to teach: Messages from a physics methods class. *Journal of Teacher Education, 45*, 86–95.

Schiro, S. M. (2013). *Curriculum theory: Conflicting visions and enduring concerns* (2nd ed). Thousand Oaks, CA: SAGE Publications, Inc.

Swedish National Agency for Education [Skolverket] (2018). *Preschool curriculum* [Läroplan för förskolan, Lpfö], 1998, and the *amended Preschool Curriculum 2010*.

Victorian Department of Education and Training (DET). (2016). *Victorian early years learning and development framework. for all children from birth to 8 years*. Melbourne, VIC: State of Victoria Department of Education and Training.

Wells, M. B., & Bergnehr, D. (2014). Families and family policies in Sweden. In M. Robila (Ed.), *Handbook of family policies across the globe* (pp. 91–107). New York: Springer.

Williams, K.M. (2017). John Dewey in the 21st Century. *Journal of Inquiry and Action in Education, 9*(1), 91–102.

Practice-based approaches to kinaesthetic learning

Katrina Allegos, Anna Crozier,
Helen Darrer, Jackie Dimattina,
Suzanne Donaghey,
Catherine Farrar, Amy Goodale,
Charmian Harris, Georgie
O'Meara and Susanne Garvis

Introduction

In this chapter, we share insights on the importance of the Reggio Emilia approach in supporting kinaesthetic learning in Early Years settings with young children. The Reggio Emilia approach has inspired Early Childhood Education across the world and is known for positive and strong child images, environments as the third teacher, the importance of relationships and the documentation (Büsra Kaynak-Ekici et al., 2021). This has led to the development of strong policies and practices within Early Childhood Education and Care to support children's learning and development.

The Hundred Languages of Children is a key pedagogical strategy within the Reggio Emilia approach. The "Hundred Language of Children enables children to express themselves in numerous ways, through projects and learning invitations" (Büsra Kaynak-Ekici et al., 2021, p. 703). This includes different ways to express thoughts and ideas, where language is also seen as endless. With this assumption, we also include kinaesthetic learning as a language. The Early Years educator, as such, takes on a role to "provoke" children to engage, think and explore (Hewett, 2001). The educator offers children materials in different ways to manipulate the physical environment, leading to curiosity and questioning by the child (Sargent, 2013). The

DOI: 10.4324/9781003268772-4

teacher can engage and support the different languages to support deeper learning by children and provide opportunities for continued reflection and questioning. This approach supports the individual needs of all children.

The role of the teacher is important in creating learning environments that allow children to engage in deep learning (Kinney & Wharton, 2008). This suggests that the teacher is aware of how the learning environment stimulates learning and provides opportunities for open-ended research by the child. The teacher is also aware of how the environment can stimulate the physical development of the child and support movement through the use of painting, dancing, music, drama and other types of movement to express knowledge and understanding. The role of the teacher is to support, observe and react to the child (Sargent, 2013) as they engage with the environment around them. This includes individually as well as collaboratively.

In this chapter, we explore the pedagogical possibilities for movement that provide opportunities for kinaesthetic learning. The chapter begins with a focus on study and methods before we move into a discussion of the key themes that emerge from the teachers' perspectives from the two case studies provided. We conclude with key messages for supporting kinaesthetic learning with children aged 3–5 years within a Reggio Emilia approach. We also discuss the importance of documenting pedagogical practice in the early years of education.

Focus of study

The focus of this study is to explore examples of kinaesthetic learning with children aged 3–5 years in an Early Years learning centre within Australia. The aim of this chapter is to provide examples of pedagogical practice and explore key themes that emerge around thinking, problem-solving and communication as part of kinaesthetic learning. Within this study, a particular focus of Reggio Emilia approach was implemented to support positive learning with young children and to foster multiple ways of representing meaning and understanding.

Methods

A qualitative study design was used where we engage in reflective writing around experiences of implementing kinaesthetic learning. As Sandelowski (2004) suggests, qualitative research is intended to create knowledge around human experience – in this case kinaesthetic movement. Through active conversations around practice, we write, inquire, feel, listen and connect (Helin, 2016). Active dialogue also provides a space to "construct new meaning that is generated together" (Smith, 2015, p. 656). The group would meet regularly (over a period of 5 months) to share, reflect and generate meaning on pedagogical practices.

The group consisted of eight educators from a private school early learning centre located in Melbourne, Australia. The educators were qualified to work in Early Childhood Education and had all worked at the early learning centre for a number of years. They had also undertaken Reggio Emilia training and regularly engaged in professional learning opportunities.

After a dialogue about how best to represent practice, two cases were found for description and reflection on learning to demonstrate pedagogical practice. The cases were organised into age ranges. Case study one consists of a three-year-old group, while case study two consists of a four-year-old group of children. Both groups had different learning projects within a Reggio Emilia foundation for learning.

Across the cases, data was analysed with thematic analysis. We implemented Braun and Clarke's (2006) six phased methods for thematic analysis. However, the process was also iterative and reflective. The researchers immersed themselves in the data so they were familiar with the breadth and depth of content (Braun & Clarke, 2006). As part of this process, we also provide a description of each theme (Braun & Clarke, 2006) to also disclose any hidden assumptions in the themes. As part of the final check, we also engaged in member checking around the respondent views and researcher representation of them (Lincoln & Guba, 1985; Tobin & Begley, 2004).

The case studies are written from the perspectives of the teacher and teaching assistants. The focus is on their observations, pictures and reflections to support meaning across and within each case study. The case studies converse multiple periods of time and show shared individual and collaborative learning experiences.

Case study 1 (3-year-old group): The image of me: Identity

The exploration of identity for the children in our K3 groups for 2022 and their families, began prior to the commencement of the school year with the inclusion of a Looking in the Mirror page in every child's orientation pack. This was to be completed over the summer break as a provocation into "Who am I? What do I look like? How do I belong?" The purpose of this learning was for the children to recognise who they are in the world and where they belong, and to acknowledge and embrace their uniqueness and that of those around them.

The Looking in the Mirror page includes an image of the child (photographic or drawn) and other images/words that reflect the child's story thus far. Every child has this page attached to their locker in the classroom and as the term progresses the children are frequently observed sharing with their friends something of their own identity.

At the beginning of term one, our focus in the classroom was to become familiar with the image of self. What do I look like? What do I see when I look at a face? How do I represent a face? This required the children's understanding of spatial relationships as they looked at where each part of the face fits in relation to another. And most importantly even though we all have the same key parts; How am I uniquely me?

> The foundational sense of who we are is profoundly important. Identity is aligned with belonging, the sense of feeling included and secure in the social settings (family, community, Early Childhood services and schools) that are part of everyday life.
> (Department of Education and Training & Victorian Curriculum Assessment Authority, 2016, p. 18)

Outcome 1 from the Victorian Early Years Learning and Development Framework is, "Children have a strong sense of identity." This directly links with the work being done with the K3's around the children's identity perceptions. This is not only an exploration of the physical but an exploration of the child's sense of belonging. By reflecting on the learning in the classroom it is vital that as educators we consider the different perspectives of each child. The Practice Principle, "Reflective Practice" supports this method of teaching and learning.

Considering that our children in K3 this year had spent the last 2 years (2/3 of their lives) in a lockdown situation due to the COVID-19 pandemic, it seemed reasonable to assume that children would have a broad spectrum of ability levels. To cater for all children, a variety of learning experiences were planned using a range of materials. Our aim as educators was to gain insight into children's identity perceptions by providing various materials for the children to explore.

Our morning meetings provided many shared learning experiences, including passing a mirror around the circle of children while singing "Looking in the Mirror Who Can I see?"; not only gave each child an introduction to the names of classmates but enabled them the time to look closely at their own image.

We also used a large hoop placed in the centre of the circle of children, along with a variety of loose parts including blocks, stones, shells, sticks, shredded paper, pine cones, as stimulus to create a face within the hoop. Children took it in turns to place something within the hoop that would help to build a face. We revisited this learning experience over quite a few days of group meetings, observing the children as they created several different-looking faces, demonstrating that we all have the same set of features, but we are all unique.

"Some people have oval faces and some people have circles" Child M, 3 years old

We continued to explore this learning in the classroom, again using loose parts but this time with a wooden circle frame placed on a round mirror, as a provocation for the children to create a face. A magnetic board with a face outline was used with magnetic parts to encourage children to form a face with more detailed features, including eyebrows and eye colour. These learning experiences developed an understanding of what needs to be included to make a face complete. Children experimented with different looks; different parts created a new set of features (see Figure 4.1).

> Tesia and me both have long hair that's the same and black eyes that's the same. My sister's legs are a bit more longer than mine.
> (Child K, 3 years old)

We also included a printing art experience, using a choice of black or white paint onto a coloured paper circle with corks, sticks and other shapes to form the parts of a face. The monochromatic approach took the focus off the pretty colours and highlighted the use of shapes to create features.

Figure 4.1 Children making faces

This learning experience was extremely popular with all children as the outcomes were very achievable.

The play dough table demonstrated some very creative and open-ended learning that occurred without provocation. Whilst sitting with a group of children and encouraging them to roll balls of dough an interesting outcome occurred. A large ball on the table prompted a child to take the small balls she was rolling and to place them on to the large ball in the area we would expect to find eyes. Then she used other dough to make hair, then a nose, then the mouth.

"Look it's a face!" Child F, 3 years old

As the children became more competent in their understanding of what was involved in creating a face we decided to experiment with mirrors and markers. Children were invited to sit in front of a mirror. What did they see? Using a marker, we encouraged them to draw themselves on the mirror, focusing on what they could see as they looked in the mirror. The results were mixed, as children with high levels of ability delighted in the mastery of looking at themselves and drawing the reflection of their face. Others found it complex and distracting, seeing themselves moving and then trying to make a still image. Some made a full image of a person with little regard for the face they were looking at.

After weeks of exploring the concept of "Identity," we set up a small table in a quiet part of the room with a mirror, white paper, and black markers. Children were invited to draw their own face. By this stage, most children were happily engaged and able to create a representation of their image.

> Creativity becomes more visible when adults try to be more attentive to the cognitive processes of children rather than to the results they achieve.
>
> (Malaguzzi, 1993)

A child may express themselves through drawing, painting, storytelling, sculpture, music, or dance. Within the Reggio principles, no method is given more value than another. As educators, we recognise the importance of individual learning and value the "process" rather than the "product" in a child's educational journey. Perhaps they are visual, auditory, or kinaesthetic learners. The "100 Languages" poem is a metaphor for the potential of children, it implores us to believe that children can express themselves in more than one way.

Intentional teaching with a variety of learning experiences ensured that all children engaged in learning. These experiences not only catered for individual interest's and learning styles but also each child's developmental stage. The children were able to demonstrate their understanding of identity, beginning with physical features by using hands-on learning to construct a face and explore the beginnings of what makes us unique and individual. Future planning will explore each child's personal identity in terms of a social and cultural context. The discovery of our own uniqueness, what we look like and where we belong is a journey that will not only continue throughout this year but over a lifetime. This is merely the beginning.

Case study 2 (4-year-old group): *How it all begins – Life Cycles*

The concept of life cycles and how living things grow and change was introduced to the K4 Pre-Prep classes through a chick-hatching programme.

This learning opportunity sought to provide children with firsthand experience of the hatching process and subsequent observation of the chick's growth and development.

Implications of the COVID-19 pandemic over the past two years meant that children had been learning in isolation. Being able to provide the children with this collaborative learning experience meant that the children and educators could work together to co-construct and build their understandings of the chicken life cycle.

Thoughtfully planned small group learning experiences were provided so that the children could experience the value of kinaesthetic learning through their senses. This encouraged the children to "experience the benefits and pleasures of shared learning exploration" (Department of Education, Employment and Workplace Relations (DEEWR), 2009, Section 4.4).

A variety of learning experiences around this unit of inquiry were offered in the classroom across a four-week period. Preliminary conversations, both whole class and smaller group, enabled educators to ascertain the children's prior knowledge. Open-ended questioning and educator prompts encouraged children to share their insights and predictions of the chick-hatching process that they were about to experience.

In preparation for the arrival of the eggs, and in recognising the "environment as the Third Teacher" (Malaguzzi, 1993), a dedicated learning space was thoughtfully designed in the "studio"; a communal learning area connecting the two classes. Projections of chickens roaming farms were used in the studio space to aid the children's understanding of where the eggs originated and enabled the children to immerse themselves in the project.

As we know:

> Active involvement builds children's understandings of concepts and the creative thinking and inquiry processes that are necessary for life-long learning.
>
> (DEEWR, 2009, p. 32)

The unit of inquiry commenced with the arrival of an incubator containing twelve eggs and a brooder box housing two chicks. These were placed at eye level, allowing children the opportunity to engage effortlessly with the eggs and chicks.

The children regularly checked on the eggs, waiting with anticipation for their hatching. Negotiations around turn-taking took place between peers, ensuring every student had the opportunity to observe what was happening in both the incubator and brooder box.

The initial moment of hatching was filmed so that it could be experienced and revisited by all. "Come on chicky, you can do it!" Child A cheered, as he watched the first chick hatch before his eyes. Subsequent hatchings were also recorded, "providing a basis for continuing discussion and further opportunities and possibilities for concept formation" (Millikan, 2003, p. 37). Many spontaneous dramatic play scenarios of chick-hatching came from revisiting these recordings (See Figure 4.2).

We drew on the philosophy of the Reggio Emilia Approach to engage The Hundred Languages of learning. Drawing, painting, sculpture and dramatic play experiences were offered to support the children's understandings. Literacy and numeracy experiences were also offered, allowing for a holistic learning experience.

Drawing materials and magnifying glasses were provided for those children eager to document what they could see and understand through

Figure 4.2 Watching eggs hatch

observational drawings. Children were given the opportunity to examine the features and characteristics of the chicks and observe the differences between the younger and older chicks. Over time, the children's drawings became more intricate and considered as they understood and observed more detail in the growing chicks.

Invitations to represent the chicken life cycle through playdough and clay were then presented to the children. By providing experiences in sculpture, the children used their hands to manipulate and mould the clay into various shapes such as chicks, hens, nests, and eggs. Rich discussions of their observations and developing understandings of the life cycle of the chicks were noted during these experiences "Its beak is so pointy," commented Child H as she manipulated the play dough to form the beak of her chick (see Figure 4.3).

Opportunities for rhyme were introduced to further support the children's ability to describe the hatching process. Inclusions of integrated hand and body movements encouraged moments for kinaesthetic and creative learning for each child. Through playful repetition, each child learned the words and corresponding actions which were recited with great enthusiasm.

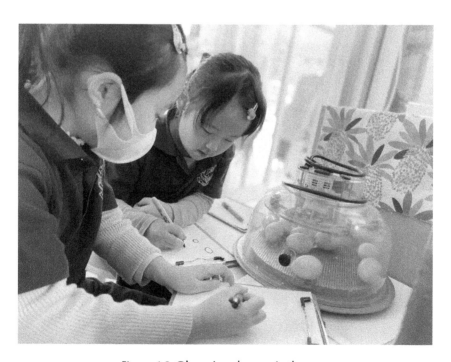

Figure 4.3 Observing changes in the eggs

Next, the children were invited to hold one of the chicks. At this point in the inquiry, the children had become more conscious of the chick's perspective and how the chicks might feel about being held. This awareness prompted action; some "rules" were agreed upon, with a collective understanding that "gentle hands" and "soft voices" were required during the handling.

The children's voices were documented during this experience:

Child A – "I can see their skin is different"

Child B – "Some chicks are the same colour"

Child C – "Some are white, and some are black"

Child D – "I can see white, black, and yellow"

Child E – "The have a beak and it has a tooth on it. It helps them break out"

Child F – "Chicks have down feathers and then they get adult feathers"

A range of fiction and non-fiction texts and ICT clips of the life cycle of the chick further strengthened the children's learnings. With this, amazing drawings and paintings were created representing the chick life cycle. Some children chose to extend their skills by labelling or numbering the sequence (Figure 4.4).

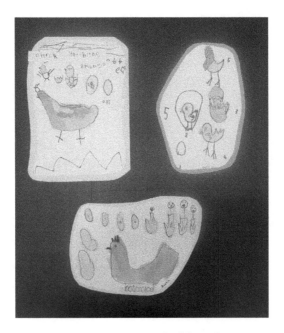

Figure 4.4 Drawing the life cycle

Two weeks after their hatching, it was time for the children to bid the chicks farewell. Many children were reluctant to say goodbye but took comfort in learning they'd be returned to their mothers at the farm.

Three hens replaced the chicks and will be tended to by the children as part of this continuing learning journey. With the hens now a permanent part of our outdoor learning environment, children will experience our interdependence with other living things as they cohabitate in the garden. Each child will have opportunities to feed the hens and collect their eggs, which will be used for cooking experiences within the early learning centre classrooms.

By engaging in this hands-on unit of inquiry, the children gained a deep understanding of the chicken life cycle. Making provisions for a programme that was inclusive of children's different learning styles was imperative to a meaningful learning outcome.

Discussion

The two case studies provided above for a three-year-old group and a four-year-old group highlight the important role of the teacher and teaching assistants in supporting a range of children's different learning styles, especially after COVID lockdowns. A key theme was a focus on intentional teaching to support varied learning experiences for children where they could engage with different elements of kinaesthetic learning to support their own and the group's learning. The adults were aware of the current understandings of children and helped scaffold them to new understandings in both case studies. The pedagogical support given took on many different elements, with the environment acting as the "third educator" for the children. A range of different languages allowed children to communicate and represent their learning, with no language being more powerful than another. As such, children were able to experience and reflect on a number of different mediums of communication and actively participate in the learning process.

Another key theme across and within the case studies was the concept of time. In both cases, time was not fixed, allowing children to engage and direct with the topic over extended periods. In both cases, the activity lasted beyond one session, with various activities afterwards leading to an extension of the learning, driven by children's engagement and interest. As such, the role of the teacher was both to direct but also observe for future direction with the learning experiences and engage in continual reflection on the overall learning process taking part. This also included the use of a variety of activities to support various kinaesthetic ways of understanding. Through this approach, the teachers were also able to demonstrate connections to the relevant learning curricula frameworks to show connections to children's learning and development. This included elements associated with identity and shared learning explorations. In particular, the adults were able to navigate a balance between individual learning and collaborative learning of children. This balance provided opportunities for further learning from each other and allowed all children to be supported in their learning and development within the early learning centre.

In both case studies, the learning experience also did not have an end (another key theme identified). In the first case, future planning would begin for exploring children's identity in social and cultural contexts. In the second case, learning continued with the introduction of three hens and the use of eggs in cooking. As such, both cases demonstrate continual reflections for future learning development and highlight the important role of involving children actively in the learning process. The adults and children may decide to continue elements of the learning across the entire year or start to blend the learning experiences in the cases into further themes or activities to be explored (such as further life cycles or constructions of identity).

These case studies also provide the opportunity to document pedagogical practice with kinaesthetic learning within the Early Childhood research community. Across the research literature, there is a lack of pedagogical practices that highlight how adults and children engage in kinaesthetic learning within Early Childhood settings. This chapter helps to fill part of this void by documenting the practices of two cases in regard to supporting children's kinaesthetic learning. The documentation allows others to reflect on pedagogical practices for kinaesthetic education and consider future possibilities for their own practices. The documentation of the case studies also shows evidence of the importance of kinaesthetic learning for young children and shows the importance of Reggio Emilia philosophy for supporting different languages of children in their communication. As such, the Early Childhood profession can benefit from reflection on such pedagogical examples to support not only children's learning but professional learning within the profession. We advocate for more sharing of pedagogical practice to build knowledge and understanding.

Conclusion

This chapter has reflected upon two case studies to explore kinaesthetic learning with young children in Early Years settings. The two examples provide opportunities for how adults have supported young children's inquiry and curiosity within the learning process. Through the foundation of Reggio Emilia, children were able to express themselves and their knowledge in multiple ways and languages, including kinaesthetic to create meaning and understanding of identity and life cycles. The adults involved allowed children to engage in a range of different mediums and learning experiences to support a variety of individual learning needs. Children were able to work together, collaboratively and engage in thinking and continual problem-solving with the notion of kinaesthetic learning. These "real world" examples show the importance of inquiry-based learning with young children and the potential for positive and supported learning experiences, based on children's interests. The examples also show the importance of intentional teaching to support and develop children's knowledge further, with continual reflection important as part of the planning cycle. Further documentation of teacher pedagogical practices in supporting young children's kinaesthetic learning is important for the Early Childhood profession and the research community. This study helps to fill this initial void by documenting pedagogical practice.

Acknowledgement

The authors would like to acknowledge the involvement of Sally Powell in developing this chapter.

References

Braun, V., & Clarke, V. (2006). Using thematic analysis in psychology. *Qualitative Research in Psychology, 3*, 77–101. doi:10.1191/1478088706qp063oa

Büsra Kaynak-Ekici, K., Merve Imir, H., & Fuyla Temel, Z. (2021). Learning invitations to Reggio Emilia approach: A case study. *Education 3–13, 49*(6), 703–715.

Department of Education, Employment and Workplace Relations (DEEWR). (2009). Being, belonging and becoming the early years learning framework for Australia. Barwon, ACT Commonwealth of Australia.

Department of Education and Training & Victorian Curriculum Assessment Authority. (2016). Victorian early years learning and development framework: for all children from birth to eight years. Department of Education and Training, Melbourne.

Helin, J. (2016). Dialogical writing: Co-inquiring between the written and the spoken word. *Culture and Organization*. doi: 10.1080/14759551.2016.1197923

Hewett, V. M. (2001). Examining the Reggio Emilia approach to early childhood education. *Early Childhood Education Journal, 29*(2), 95–100.

Kinney, L., & Wharton, P. (2008). *An encounter with Reggio Emilia: Children's early learning made visible*. New York, NY: Routledge.

Lincoln, Y., & Guba, E.G. (1985). *Naturalistic inquiry*. Newbury Park, CA: Sage.

Malaguzzi, L. (1993). For an education based on relationships. *Young Children, 49*(1), 9–12.

Millikan, J. (2003). *Reflections: Reggio Emilia principles within Australian contexts*. Sydney, NSW: Pademelon Press.

Sandelowski, M. (2004). Using qualitative research. *Qualitative Health Research, 14*, 1366–1386.

Sargent, M. (2013). *The project approach: Creativity in the early years. A practical guide to developing a child-centered curriculum*. London: Practical Pre-School Books.

Smith, D. (2015). Exploring interprofessional collaboration and ethical practice: A story of emancipatory professional learning. *Reflective Practice, 16*(5), 652–676.

Tobin, G.A., & Begley, C.M. (2004). Methodological rigour within a qualitative framework. *Journal of Advanced Nursing, 48*, 388–396. doi:10.1111/j.1365-2648.2004.03207.x

A kinaesthetic approach to teaching mathematics education in the early years

Bin Wu and Wendy Goff

Introduction

Young children's mathematics learning has recently received increased worldwide attention from scholars and society (Wright, 2021). The reason for this attention is two-fold. First, early mastery of mathematical concepts is viewed as necessary for children's later mathematical learning and development. Second, research confirms that very young children can use and engage in abstract reasoning about mathematics in sophisticated ways (MacDonald, 2018). These views raise a question of how to nurture young children's engagement in the higher-order thinking of mathematical concepts through play, whilst traditionally children's free play has been reconsidered as contradictory to adult intervention (see Pyle et al., 2017).

In Australia, Early Childhood Education adopts a play-based learning approach. Play, as defined in the Early Years Learning Framework for Australia (Department of Education and Training [DET], 2017) provides "a context for learning through which children organise and make sense of their social worlds, as they engage actively with people, objects and representations" (p. 48). Subsequently, the kinaesthetic learning of mathematics is in effect, embedded in EC mathematics education as a multisensory experience that supports children to make sense of what they encounter (Wager, 2013). However, influenced by Cartesian dualism, there is a deep-seated binary assumption of body and mind. Hence, kinaesthetic activities are not valued as learning or are considered to be at

DOI: 10.4324/9781003268772-5

the periphery and a supplement to cognitive development. However spontaneous sensory experiences are not always harnessed or recognised by Early Childhood educators as mathematical learning. Free play alone is not always sufficient for young children to grasp scientific ideas (Fleer & Hobson, 2012) including mathematical concepts. To effectively support the kinaesthetic learning of mathematics embedded in children's play, Early Childhood educators need to understand these creative, multi-sensory experiences through play and how they support and build young children's mathematical learning.

In this chapter, we discuss the importance of kinaesthetic learning in mathematics education by focusing on how children engage with mathematics in creative and multi-sensory ways. Guided by Bloom's notion of learning for mastery (1968) and Vygotsky's (1978) Zone of Proximal Development, we present a framework that supports Early Childhood educators to identify, assist, nurture and build on the kinaesthetic learning experiences embedded in children's mathematical play. We then use the framework to explicate the teaching and learning process and demonstrate how educators might plan for mathematics teaching and learning in multi-sensory ways. The framework aims to reconcile and integrate tensions in young children's mathematic learning through kinaesthetic play: between abstract learning and concrete play and between developmental and academic needs. The chapter concludes by underlining how kinaesthetic teaching and learning of mathematics might be supported across and between the contexts of children's play.

Literature review

Before starting school, children's bodily or kinaesthetic interactions with the world around them are critical to their learning and development. Children use their bodies to experiment with ideas, progress, enhance and advance their thinking. In fact, "learners are simultaneously sensorimotor bodies, reflective minds, and social beings" (Nguyen & Larson, 2015, p. 342). Therefore, it is not surprising that young children come to sense, know, and engage with academic learning long before they experience any formal education and schooling.

This is the same with mathematics learning. It has been well-established that young children's mathematical understanding occurs prior to any formal mathematics instruction takes place (MacDonald et al., 2016). Such engagement and learning are supported by young children's developing language as well as their kinaesthetic and bodily experiences and interactions with others and environments. For example, children might use their fingers for counting; their bodies to repeat or recognise patterns; or they may align an oral chant of the forward number system with the steps they walk along a path or down a staircase. Similarly, children might use their bodies to express, represent and learn about size, length, speed, and quantity as they interact within their everyday environments.

Despite what we know about children's sensory experiences with mathematics in the years before school, kinaesthetic and bodily learning in mathematics has not been extensively explored. In 2000, Lakoff and Núñez suggested that studies that have focused on gesture and gesture/speech provided some good empirical support for the kinaesthetic and embodied nature of mathematical knowledge. They recommended that more work was necessary to understand how this could be harnessed to support mathematical learning (Lakoff & Núñez, 2000).

Since 2000, research on gestures in mathematics education has provided critical insight into the role of gestures to support mathematics learning, particularly in supporting understanding through human interactions and oral communications (Arzarello, Robutti, Paola, & Sabena, 2009; Edwards, 2009; Yoon, Thomas, & Dreyfus, 2011). It is now widely accepted that gesture can assist children in problem-solving (Yoon, Thomas, & Dreyfus, 2011) and is a valuable tool for supporting the understanding of mathematical questions and questioning (Edwards, 2009). Nonetheless, research into young children's kinaesthetic and bodily experiences and how they can support young children's mathematical understandings remains sparse. This poses questions about how young children's early bodily and kinaesthetic experiences with mathematics might be enhanced or harnessed in the years before school, particularly in Early Years settings.

Another question concerns the adult's role and the content of learning in children's kinaesthetic learning. While consensus in the literature is that play, providing contexts for hands-on and body-movement learning, is a natural and proximal modality for young children to acquire and master mathematics concepts and thinking, without explicit teaching and guidance, spontaneous play alone does not autonomically result in abstract thinking which is an essential requirement for mastering scientific concepts (Fleer & Hoban, 2012). Unstructured kinaesthetic activities by themselves are insufficient for young children to grasp mathematical meanings (Anthony & Walshaw, 2009; van Oers, 2010). For example, when they wipe the table, children do not autonomically comprehend the mathematical notion of areas as adults might have assumed (McLachlan et al., 2013). Scientific concepts need to be explicitly taught because they "are explanatory inventions, their genesis does not arise in everyday situations without explanation or conscious exploration" (Fleer & Hoban, 2012, p. 62). In practice, this suggests that children need to progress from concrete experience to abstract or higher-order thinking in mastering scientific concepts (Fleer, 2011). That is, moving from informal (experiential learning and everyday concepts) to formal learning (using formal mathematic language). Teachers' role is to mediate these two ends to support children's conceptual development through intentional teaching (McLachlan et al., 2013). Barwell (2016) cautions that children do not move from informal to formal learning through linear pathways. Instead, they work with adults to "expand the repertoire of possible ways to make meaning in mathematics" (p. 331).

Moreover, mathematics learning is a sociocultural practice that should be understood within its context. Hence mathematics learning is a dynamic and complex process rather than static. For example, China and the US have different approaches to teaching young children mathematics. The Chinese instructional approach highlights "a high degree of intentional teaching and age-specific content coverage" when the teaching practice in the US stresses children's interests and yet teachers' subject knowledge is not always evident. The difference between the two cultures presents "the competing forces in Early Childhood Education: children's interest-driven curriculum and subject-driven curriculum. Both positions may play important roles" (Li et al., 2015, p. 21). This observation reflects a perspective as well as a reality in practice where content teaching is not detached from children's interests, and attending to children's interests does not contradict a focus on content teaching. As Ginsburg (2006) noted, mathematics may be positioned differently in children's play: mathematics embedded in play, play centring on mathematics, and play with the mathematics that has been taught. Further, both adults' intentional teaching and children's interest-driven learning are observed in children's play. Pyle and Danniels (2017) maintained that teachers' roles in play-based learning constitute a continuum from teacher-directed instruction to child-initiated unstructured play. In short, "the research community seems to have embraced multiple perspectives, simultaneously acknowledging individual, social, and cultural influences on mathematical thought" (Newton & Alexander, 2013, p. 24).

In contrast to the dynamic nature of children's mathematics learning as discussed above, in Anglophone literature of Early Childhood Education, there are deep-rooted binary assumptions about children's play and mathematics teaching and learning: adults' intentional teaching versus children's interest (see Edwards, 2017; Pyle & Danniels, 2017); content-driven versus learner-centred curricula (Li et al., 2015); and learning for development versus academic achievements (see Pyle et al., 2017). Indeed, the body-and-mind dualism poses a curricular challenge in teaching and learning (Craig et al., 2013). The binary prepositions are stemmed from the Cartesian dualism that conjectures the split between the mind and the body, and subsequently, the self and others, and the individuals and environments, play and learning.

In summary, in a play-based environment mandated in a Western liberal Early Childhood curriculum, kinaesthetic learning is a *de facto* medium for teaching and learning. However, due to a sociocultural influence of Cartesian dualism, some in-grained assumptions about young children's kinaesthetic learning are binary in nature. These dichotomous presuppositions hinder the rich opportunities that a kinaesthetic learning environment provides. Because of an entrenched belief that places adults' teaching as opposing a child-centred approach, there is a "need to provide early-childhood educators with pedagogical play-based models that can support children's conceptual development" where educators play a more intentional and active role in children's play (Lewis et al., 2019, p. 17). To address the issues above, in the following section, we propose a holistic instructional model of teaching mathematics learning through play where children routinely engage in multiple modalities simultaneously, such as visual, audio, and kinaesthetic.

Theoretical framework and instructional model

Considering the views expressed above, we propose an instructional model for kinaesthetic mathematical learning in the context of play. Broadly, the framework is underpinned by Vygotsky's (1987) concept of the Zone of Proximal Development. At the instructional level, it adopts a modified mastery learning approach. The instructional model (see Table 5.1) features a

Table 5.1 Integrated framework

Instructional strategies (Fisher et al., 2016, pp. 81–82)	Integrated framework (Wu & Goff, 2021)
Focused instruction (I do it) *during which the teacher establishes the learning intention and uses modelling and demonstrating to show how skills and concepts are utilised.*	**Demonstration** *where concepts are purposefully designed and demonstrated by teachers.*
Guided instruction (We do it) *during which the teacher uses questions, prompts, and cues to scaffold student learning.* **Collaborative learning (You do it together)** *during which students work with peers to take on sufficiently complex tasks in order to consolidate understanding.*	**Exploration** *where educators and children explore new or old concepts in relation to children's existing knowledge.*
Independent learning (You do it alone) *during which students practice and apply what they have learned, now equipped with the cognitive resources they need to engage in self-directed tasks.*	**Application** *where the emphasis is on children applying their knowledge and skills in different contexts.*

continuum of teachers' and learners' responsibility in the context of play to balance the need for deliberate teaching and children's meaning-making through kinaesthetic exploration.

The model incorporates a continuum from teacher-led targeted instruction, to guided instruction and collaborative learning to complete independent learning (Fisher et al., 2016) and different types of play: exploration, demonstration, and application (Wu & Goff, 2021). We will first discuss Vygotsky's theory that underpins the proposed model. From the theory, we will proceed to discuss its implications for practice, and finally the proposed instruction model.

For Vygotsky, cognitive development is sociocultural and learning is interdependent between the child and environments. "Vygotskian cultural-historical theory of human development, by invoking dialectical logic, has transcended Cartesian substance dualism and in turn has proffered a monistic and process-anchored ontology for emerging becoming of human consciousness" (Karimi-Aghdam, 2017, p. 76). A key concept in Vygotsky's theory is the Zone of Proximal Development (ZPD). Eun (2019) argued that the ZPD should be used as an overarching concept to synthesise Vygotsky's theory. In this chapter, our proposed instructional model is based on Eun's (2019) suggestion.

The ZPD is defined as "the distance between the actual developmental level as determined by independent problem solving and the level of potential development as determined through problem-solving under adult guidance or in collaboration with more capable peers" (Vygotsky, 1978 p. 86). This concept emphasises the social interactions and interdependence between the learner and the environment and the collaborative nature of teaching and learning (Eun, 2019). Chaykin (2003) observed three common assumptions of the ZPD and their criticisms. The first is the generality assumption. It is assumed that the concept is applicable to teaching and learning all subject matters. However, the emphasis is on the child's development rather than subject-specific instructions, which in turn, should be based on the child's overall development. The second is the assistance assumption. That is, a less competent learner requires assistance from a more competent peer or adult support. Nonetheless, the key is not so much how competent the peer or adult is, rather it stresses the interactions between the two. The third is the potentiality assumption. A primary concern of this assumption is the property of the potential. Whereas the ZPD refers to the child's potential for future development, "the potential is not a property of the child – as these formulations are sometimes interpreted – but simply an indication of the presence of certain maturing functions, which can be a target for mean-ingful, interventive action" (p. 43). Chaykin's (2003) clarification of the three assumptions reiterates the sociocultural and collaborative nature of learning and teaching as a tenet in Vygotsky's theory. Due to Vygotsky's premature death, many questions about the implementation of the ZPD in education are still unanswered. Despite this, the ZPD has inspired further research and subsequent application in practice. In the following, based on the ZPD con-cept, we present an instructional model by merging teaching strategies of scaffolding and mastery learning.

Scaffolding and mastery learning

A well-known and widely practised strategy drawn from the ZPD is scaffolding. Vygotsky did not use the term directly but implied its practice as the ZPD alludes to "what the child is able to do in collaboration today he will be able to do independently tomorrow" (Vygotsky, 1978, p. 211). Along this line, Wood, Burner and Ross (1976) developed and defined scaffolding as a process "that enables a child or novice to solve a task or achieve a goal that would be beyond his unassisted efforts" (p. 90). Specifically, scaffolding is a process from teacher taking full responsibility, to more collaborative learning and eventual learner's independent learning. Instructional strategies include the four components of focused instruction, guided instruction, collaborative learning, and independent learning. Put simply, the four components could be expressed from the teacher's perspective, as "I do, we do it, you do it together, and you do it alone" (Fisher et al., 2016, p. 82). These four elements are generic scaffolding instructions that can be adopted in a play-based learning. For example, in Wu and Goff's (2021) integrated pedagogical framework in play, the *demonstration* phase incorporates focused instruction. Guided instruction and collaborative learning that encourage peers and teachers to collaborate in learning are implicit in the *exploration* phase. In the *application* phase where children are encouraged to practise what they have learned across a range of situations is parallel to independent learning. Unlike schools where lessons are relatively structured, learning in Early Childhood settings is a mixture of both spontaneous and planned experiences. In addition, as mentioned earlier, children's mastery of mathematical concepts does not follow a linear pathway (Barwell, 2016). Hence the process of scaffolding should not be treated as rigid or fixed. In light of what play affords, Wu and Goff (2021) recommended that the different phases are used with different combinations and orders.

While the term scaffolding has been widely used in education, the question remains, how do we know about children's zone of proximal development? To explain this question, we incorporate the concept of mastery learning. A mastery approach emphasises in-depth learning by breaking down tasks into manageable sequential steps and constant feedback.

> By definition, mastery learning is a method of instruction where the focus is on the role of feedback in learning … through one or more trials, students have to achieve a specified level of content knowledge prior to progression to the next unit of instruction.
>
> (Motamedi & Sumrall, 2000, p. 32)

Mastery learning is based on the premise that all learners can master the subject matter given appropriate coaching. When teaching the same concept to a group, the teacher will constantly assess each learner and use differentiated strategies until the concepts are mastered before moving to the next step (Guskey, 1980). In this way, the ZPD is negotiated through feedback and interaction between the teacher, the child, and among peers. In ECEC, a mathematical concept can be broken down into manageable components. Through the four instructional strategies (Fishers et al., 2016) and constant receiving and giving feedback, each component of the concept can be actively explored and mastered. We will illustrate this point with practical examples in the next section.

From theory to practice

Number sense in mathematics provides an ideal example from which to demonstrate how kinaesthetic learning and the bodily exploration of mathematics can support children's mathematical learning. Number sense refers to a person's ability to "understand numbers and number relationships and to solve mathematical problems that are not bound by traditional algorithms" (Bobis, 1996, p. 2). There are three components of number sense: number knowledge, counting and arithmetic operations (Yilmaz, 2017).

Children engage with and develop each component of number sense before they start school. It lays the foundations essential for future mathematical learning. Indeed, now several longitudinal studies suggest young children's number sense is a strong predictor of later mathematical achievement (Jordan et al., 2010; Jordan et al., 2007). The three components of number sense are embedded in children's day-to-day living. As children come to explore their worlds, they are developing number knowledge, engaging in various counting opportunities, and are performing arithmetic operations. Children develop number knowledge and counting skills because numbers are embedded in their daily lives. Similarly, children's play experiences offer various opportunities for performing arithmetic operations as children determine quantities, share, and engage in day-to-day life.

Although children naturally engage in developing their number sense and most children start school with some understanding of number sense (Yilmaz, 2017), educator input into this area of mathematics in the years before school might better support this understanding because scientific concepts need to be explicitly taught (Fleer & Hoban, 2012). Drawing on a kinaesthetic pedagogical approach when providing this support recognises the importance of play in developing children's conceptual understandings of mathematics. The integrated framework presented in the previous section provides a vehicle to support this.

Applying the integrated framework in developing and supporting children's understandings of number sense might initially involve the educator deliberately planning out different ways that children's understandings can be developed throughout the day. This might include planning out formal demonstrations of how numbers might be represented through quantity, such as reading a story to the children and inviting different children up in front of the class to demonstrate physical-bodily representations of numbers, for example, three trees blowing in the wind. Or it might involve embedding some less-formal opportunities for demonstration into the daily routine, for example, counting out loud as fruit is dished into bowls at snack time.

Educators would then build on these demonstrations through children's play experiences. This might involve the educator taking on the role of player and leading children's play as they continue to focus on supporting children's understanding of number sense. In the outdoor environment, this might include modelling and encouraging counting out loud as children manoeuvre their way through a set of stepping-stones, it might involve leading a game where a number is called out and children are required to physically create that number with their peers (e.g., a group of three children). In the indoor environment, it might be the inclusion of number cards at the art table and supporting the children to choose a number and create a set of objects that represent this number, for example three clay snakes.

The final component of the integrated framework sees educators shift their focus towards the physical environment by providing opportunities for children to apply their understandings in different ways. This is an important component of the framework as it also offers educators an opportunity to observe and assess children's developing understandings as they engage with their everyday worlds. This might involve incorporating number cards in the outdoor environment and observing how children interact with these cards. It might involve setting up a reading corner in the indoor environment with books that have numerical representations and observing how children interact with these resources.

Kinaesthetic and bodily experiences not only provide a natural vehicle for differentiation and inclusion by broadening and deepening children's cognitive understandings about number sense in different ways, but kinaesthetic and bodily teaching also provides educators with an authentic way to build on children's natural play experiences and investigations of the world around them. The integrated framework presented in this chapter supports educators to engage in this work. Let us now consider George climbing and how 1:1 support might be provided to young children through the integrated model.

An educator who has been exploring measurement or number with children in the indoor environment might take the opportunity to support George to apply his learning in a different context. As George climbs, he is physically exploring measurement, if he counts the steps he climbs, he will also be physically exploring number and the forward number sequence. The integrated framework provides a way for the educator to help George apply his mathematical understandings in a different context, in this instance the educator's role as George climbs is to talk about and use the language of mathematics. For example, counting out loud as George climbs the steps will help him to apply his understandings about the forward number sequence in the outdoor environment. Or the educator might guide George's attention toward measurement by saying things such as "You are getting further and further away from the ground George", or "You are taller than me now George", or "You are almost as tall as the tree". Climbing is a wonderful vehicle for the application of mathematics learning. It also provides a way for children to physically embody and "feel" mathematics. Educators play an important role in guiding and facilitating this learning. In fact, their explicit guidance helps children connect their kinetic experiences to higher-order thinking. Without adults' scaffolding, abstract thinking in young children might not always autonomically occur. Meanwhile, as shown in the photo, little George's bodily movements provide a context for fostering higher-order thinking skills and strategies.

Conclusion

In a play-based learning context, mathematics learning is embedded in multi-sensory exploration including kinaesthetic movements. Although a holistic approach to learning and development is often adopted by various curriculum documents, there are many entrenched divides in practices such as adults' intention vs children's learning, free play versus learning, the dualism of body versus mind. Another related issue is that children's grasp of scientific concepts does not always naturally occur but requires deliberate teaching and coaching. Because of the body-and-mind dualism, natural kinaesthetic experience is not always harnessed or recognised by Early Childhood educators as mathematical learning. To address this gap, drawing on Bloom's notion of learning for mastery (1968) and Vygotsky's (1978) notion of Zone of Proximal Development, we present a framework that supports Early Childhood educators to identify, support, nurture, and build on the kinaesthetic learning experiences embedded in children's mathematical play. We have also illustrated how the framework could be applied in practice. The aim of the framework is to break down dichotomies of free play and intentional teaching, abstract thinking, and bodily movements and move towards a holistic approach to mathematics education in Early Childhood.

References

Anthony, G., & Walshaw, M. (2009). Mathematics education in the early years: Building bridges. *Contemporary Issues in Early Childhood, 10*(2), 107–121.

Arzarello, F., Paola, D., Robutti, O., & Sabena, C. (2009). Gestures as semiotic resources in the mathematics classroom. *Educational Studies in Mathematics, 70*, 97–109.

Barwell, R. (2016). Formal and informal mathematical discourses: Bakhtin and Vygotsky, dialogue and dialectic. *Educational Studies in Mathematics, 92*(3), 331–345.

Bloom, B. S. (1968). Learning for mastery. *Evaluation Comment (UCLA-CSIEP), 1*(2), 1–12.

Bobis, J. (1996). Visualisation and the development of number sense with kindergarten children. In J. Mulligan & M. Mitchelmore (Eds.), *Children's Number Learning: A Research Monograph of the Mathematics Education Group of Australasia and the Australian Association of Mathematics Teachers* (pp. 17–33). Adelaide: AAMT.

Chaiklin, S. (2003). The zone of proximal development in Vygotsky's analysis of learning and instruction In A. Kozulin, B. Gindis, V. S. Ageyev, & S. M. Miller (Eds.), *Vygotsky's educational theory in cultural context* (pp. 39–64). Cambridge: Cambridge University Press.

Craig, C. J., You, J., & Oh, S. (2013). Collaborative curriculum making in the physical education vein: a narrative inquiry of space, activity and relationship. *Journal of Curriculum Studies, 45*(2), 169–197.

Department of Education and Training [DET] (2017). The early years learning framework for Australia. Retrieved from https://docs.education.gov.au/node/2632

Edwards, L. D. (2009). Gestures and conceptual integration in mathematical talk. *Educational Studies in Mathematics, 70*, 127–141.

Edwards, S. (2017). Play-based learning and intentional teaching: Forever different? *Australasian Journal of Early Childhood, 42*(2), 4–11.

Eun, B. (2019). The zone of proximal development as an overarching concept: A framework for synthesizing Vygotsky's theories. *Educational Philosophy and Theory, 51*(1), 18–30.

Fisher, D., Frey, N., & Hite, S. A. (2016). *Intentional and targeted teaching: A framework for teacher growth and leadership.* Alexandria, Virginia: Association for Supervision & Curriculum Development.

Fleer, M. (2011). "Conceptual Play": Foregrounding imagination and cognition during concept formation in early years education. *Contemporary Issues in Early Childhood, 12*(3), 224–240.

Fleer, M., & Hoban, G. (2012). Using "Slowmation" for intentional teaching in early childhood centres: Possibilities and imaginings. *Australasian Journal of Early Childhood, 37*(3), 61–70.

Ginsburg, H. P. (2006). Mathematical play and playful mathematics: A guide for early education. In D. G. Singer, R. M. Golinkoff, & K. Hirsh-Pasek (Eds.), *Play = learning: How play motivates and enhances children's cognitive and social-emotional growth* (pp. 145–165). Oxford University Press.

Guskey, T. R. (1980). Mastery learning: Applying the theory. *Theory into Practice, 19*(2), 104–111.

Jordan, N. C., Glutting, J., & Ramineni, C. (2010). The importance of number sense to mathematics achievement in first and third grades. Learning and *Individual Differences, 20*(2), 82–88.

Jordan, N. C., Kaplan, D., Locuniak, M. N., & Ramineni, C. (2007). Predicting first-grade math achievement from developmental number sense trajectories. Learning Disabilities Research & Practice, 22(1), 36–46.

Karimi-Aghdam, S. (2017). Zone of Proximal Development (ZPD) as an emergent system: A dynamic systems theory perspective. *Integrative Psychological and Behavioral Science, 51*, 76–93.

Lakoff, G., & Núñez, R. E. (2000). *Where mathematics comes from: How the embodied mind brings mathematics into being.* New York: Basic Books.

Lewis, R., Fleer, M., & Hammer, M. (2019). Intentional teaching: Can early-childhood educators create the conditions for children's conceptual development when following a child-centred programme? *Australasian Journal of Early Childhood*, *44*(1), 6–18.

Li, X., Chi, L., DeBey, M., & Baroody, A. J. (2015). A study of early childhood mathematics teaching in the United States and China. *Early Education and Development*, *26*(3), 1–29.

MacDonald, A. (2018). *Mathematics in early childhood education*. (1st ed.) Melbourne: Oxford University Press Australia and New Zealand.

Macdonald, A., Goff, W., Dockett, S., & Perry, B. (2016). *Mathematics Education in the Early Years*. 10.1007/978-981-10-1419-2_9.

McLachlan, C., Edwards, S., & Fleer, M. (2013). *Early childhood curriculum: Planning, assessment and implementation (2 ed.)*. Melbourne: Cambridge University.

Motamedi, V., & Sumrall, W. (2000). Mastery Learning and Contemporary Issues in Education. Contemporary Issues in Education, Action in Teacher *Education*, *22*(1), 32–42.

Newton, K. J., & Alexander, P. A. (2013). Early mathematics learning in perspective: Eras and forces of change. In L. D. English & J. T. Mulligan (Eds.), *Reconceptualizing early mathematics learning* (pp. 5–28). New York: Springer.

Nguyen, D. J., & Larson, J. B. (2015). Don't forget about the body: exploring the curricular possibilities of embodied pedagogy. *Innovative Higher Education, 40*, 331–344.

Pyle, A., & Danniels, E. (2017). A Continuum of play-based learning: The role of the teacher in play-based pedagogy and the Fear of hijacking play. *Early Education and Development*, *28*(3), 274–289.

Pyle, A., De Luca, C., & Danniels, E. (2017). A scoping review of research on play-based pedagogies in kindergarten education. *Review of Education*, *5*(3), 311–351.

van Oers, B. (2010). Emergent mathematical thinking in the context of play. *Educational Studies in Mathematics, 74*, 23–37.

Vygotsky, L. (1978). *Mind in society: The development of higher psychological processes*. Cambridge, MA: Harvard University Press.

Wager, A. A. (2013). Practices that support mathematics learning in a play-based classroom. In L. D. English & J. T. Mulligan (Eds.), *Early mathematics learning in perspective: Eras and forces of change* (pp. 163–181). London: Springer.

Wood, D., Bruner, J., & Ross, G. (1976). The role of tutoring in problem solving. *Journal of Child Psychology and Child Psychiatry, 17*, 89–100.

Wright, P. (2021). Transforming mathematics classroom practice through participatory action research. *J Math Teacher Educ 24*, 155–177. https://doi.org/10.1007/s10857-019-09452-1

Wu, B., & Goff, W. (2021). Learning intentions: a missing link to intentional teaching? Towards an integrated pedagogical framework. *Early Years: An International Research Journal*. https://doi.org/10.1080/09575146.2021.1965099

Yilmaz, Z. (2017). Young children's number sense development: Age related complexity across cases of three children. *International Electronic Journal of Elementary Education*, 9(4), 891–902.

Yoon, C., Thomas, M. O., & Dreyfus, T. (2011). Grounded blends and mathematical gesture spaces: Developing mathematical understandings via gestures. Educational Studies in *Mathematics*, *78*, 371–393.

An investigation of the use of arts-based embodied learning in Early Years classrooms

Marthy Watson and
Nicole Delaney

Introduction

A class of Year 2 children puzzle over how a small caterpillar might emerge from its tiny egg. Arms are tucked in tight while bodies curl as small as they can, then roll and press against the floor. The caterpillars are too large for the only home they have known, and it is time to leave. There is no choice, they must go. As the music of Bach's Cello Suite, No. 1 (G major) shifts, the children respond. Shoulders lift, arms thrust upwards and extend, and heads emerge. "Caterpillar voices" express fears and excitement about leaving the egg and making their way into the world. The children's teacher has fun with the movements, describing the "ooching and mooching" as with still heads, the backs of the newly emerged caterpillars arch, feet wriggle, and knees tuck in snugly beneath their bodies before stretching out full length once more. The caterpillars sneak a look around as if to check if their experience of hatching is the same as others.

What children do in the classroom is not separate from the real world (Shor & Freire, 1987). The experience of the children described in the above extract exemplifies the use of embodied learning through an arts-based experience using music and dance to make meaning of their world. This inquiry lesson began with questions and a provocation. The children were asked to imagine how it might feel to be a tiny caterpillar on the verge of

DOI: 10.4324/9781003268772-6

emerging from its egg. They were asked to imagine what it would do and how it would move their body in an entirely different space to the one they had known all its life. In this experience, the children arrange and assemble movements to compose and decode meaning. Through this collective experience and movement, they found empathy and a capacity within their bodies to imagine and respond as they learn.

Our interest in arts-based practice led us to investigate the space where the arts curriculum is enacted in schools in the Foundation to Year 2. The broader project investigated how the *Australian Curriculum: The Arts Foundation to Year 10* (Australian Assessment and Reporting Authority [ACARA], n.d.) is enacted in practice in primary classrooms in Queensland. The project involved a mix of 14 urban, rural and remote primary schools across school sectors in Queensland. Initially, 26 classroom and specialist arts teachers were interviewed to look inward and reflect on their experiences enacting the arts curriculum in their classrooms. These interviews and classroom observations were done over three months and involved long car trips to regional and rural communities and school visits in the inner-city suburbs. We interviewed generalist primary school teachers and specialist arts teachers and spent time in classrooms to see how arts-based and embodied practices were integrated into this space.

In this chapter, we draw on our observations during the project to report on how embodiment is used in Early Years classrooms in Queensland, Australia. We reflect on how embodied learning through arts-based practices assists the learner in constructing knowledge and meaning from the learning experiences encountered in the classroom. Through vignettes, we highlight the different ways in which embodiment appears in and between sequences of activities. Sometimes it was visible in isolation and other times, it presented itself fluidly across and within learning experiences. We captured the teachers' reflections in vignettes to show how embodiment is used in the classroom and demonstrate various approaches and understandings of how teachers view using embodied arts-based activities for learning.

Mind vs body

For a long time, learning as a social activity in the Western world was grounded in traditional principles that follow a mentalistic educational approach that separates the mind from the body (Merleau-Ponty, 2012;

Stolz, 2015; Vaesen, 2014). The Cartesian view of the mind versus the body dichotomy has been debated by many philosophers throughout the ages, with some believing that the body does not contribute in any form to cognitive processes and that cognition is strictly a brain activity (Macedonia, 2019). This mindset though, is not limited to the past and even in the 20th century, Fodor's (1983; 2006) work on language and the mind concluded that the mind consists of a series of computational modes and that these modes are separate from each other, only controlled by a central mechanism. Similarly, Chomsky (1995) considered language as innate and existing without external influences. This could be seen as an abstract phenomenon of the mind and did not acknowledge a role for the body in cognitive processes.

Research and debate in the 20th century challenged the separation of body and mind. As early as 1934, educational scholars such as Dewey argued a connection between affect and cognition to enhance empathy. He argued that learning takes place in the perpetual and constantly evolving nexus of body, mind, and experience. Piaget (1951) described the connection between body and mind in children's learning as a process whereby the development of concepts follows action. Concepts are learned through sensory experiences. Through the arts, movement and activity are "fundamentally linked" to feeling and emotion (Wright, 2003). Embodied learning has been defined as "learning that joins body and mind in a physical and mental act of knowledge construction" (Nguyen & Larsen, 2015, p. 332) and gives "meaning to our reality" (O'Toole, 2012, p. 7).

Embodied learning

This renewed interest in embodiment has given way to an epistemological shift to challenge the traditional Cartesian view of the separation of body and mind. Despite the slow uptake to recognise the link between cognition and embodied learning, there is a growing body of evidence showing that bodily engagements play a role in children's cognitive and academic outcomes (Bresler, 2013; Eisner, 2002; Gardiner, 1993). Embodied learning is based on the idea that an inevitable link between body and mind requires the body's involvement and cognitive expression. Block and Kisssell (2001) stated that embodied knowing is "the ability to interact with a thought or an experience holistically that involves the integrated power network [neural elements, efforts, memory, language, perception and attunement of the total person]" (p. 8). Merleau-Ponty (1964) argued that embodiment is central to our consciousness and self and that through kinaesthetic awareness, children develop a sense of self and understand how perceptions, movements and emotions are intertwined. Therefore, these sensorimotor activities and the emotional involvement of the student are principal modes of embodiment (Kosmas et al., 2019). This integration of embodied learning provides opportunities for students to develop social skills and relationships with others and improve self-confidence as they work collaboratively in group settings (Ewing, 2020).

Embodied learning has made its way into many educational settings and supports the tenet that embodied learning underpins cognition to create new learning opportunities. A significant and increasing body of research, scholarship and professional practice reports on how children use embodiment to understand, learn and make sense of their world. In mathematics, researchers have linked education and neurocognitive research to show how using movement – action and gesture – can be used as a powerful tool to learn and understand content (Solyu et al., 2018). For example, early experiences with finger counting and relating fingers to numbers lay a foundation for number concepts and later skills (Solyu et al., 2018). Broadening pedagogical practices in mathematics through creative and body-based learning has positively enhanced student engagement, confidence and learning (Rankin et al., 2021). They also argued that inviting students into the learning process encouraged participation previously missing in maths lessons.

Research in language learning and reading revealed how children embodied text when reading multimodal text. These children used ritual, singing, movement and dramatisation to make sense of the text (Enriquez, 2015; Macedonia, 2014; Shin, 2017). Using multiple modes of expression in the classroom assists children in understanding the story. Moreover, if children can use visual, aural and gestural modes, it allows for a more "collaborative and personalised approach" to promote transformative learning in the classroom (Barton & Baguley, 2014, p. 105). Children that are multimodally literate use skills such as critical thinking, problem-solving and ethical thinking to process learning more effectively (Greene, 1995).

The recent development of technologies that require human physical interactions and bodily movements has highlighted the use of embodied learning in various learning contexts. Examples of this type of learning are motion-based computer games (Ayala et al., 2013). Studies into this emerging type of gaming showed a strong connection between movement and learning. They suggested that this interaction with technology can improve children's functioning and academic performance (Choa et al., 2013; Mueller et al., 2011). Studies into special education have shown that these games enhanced physical gains and social and mental health benefits (Donnelly & Lambourne, 2011; Kosmas et al., 2018; Mueller et al., 2011). However, our interest and this chapter focus on how arts-based practices appear as embodied learning in the Early Years classroom.

Arts-based practice

According to Eisner (2002), artistic practices connect the mind and body and help us to make meaning and interpret the world around us. He argued that meaning is not limited to what words can express and that using arts-based practices in classrooms can provide a way through which alternative teaching methods can assist embodied learning. Moreover, arts-based practices "not only develop imagination and creativity but also support complex understandings through divergent and lateral thinking" (Rigney et al., 2020, p. 1163). When children embody imagination and creativity, as Dewey (1934) suggested, they use their bodies, affect (feeling, emotion and mood), and aesthetic modes to engage with learning. This means that embodiment opens spaces for dialogue, individual and collaborative engagement and allows students to "notice what there is to be noticed" (Greene, 2001, p. 6).

The art forms such as drama, music, and dance create opportunities for children to engage through visual, spatial, and aural modes to generate purposeful movement. When using the arts as the vehicle for embodiment, the body becomes an active medium for learning. Children use all their body parts (including the brain) to store and distribute information. As children juxtapose their bodies to other bodies in the classroom using a gestural, visual and spatial mode, they interact with each other and co-construct a shared experience where meaning is created. Whitemore et al. (2015) worked in a Reggio Emilia pre-school to determine embodied engagement in classroom activity and reported that students read each other's bodies to make sense of their world and form connections with one another to complete tasks.

For children, it is a natural go-to to use their bodies to express themselves. Teachers can use these modes to articulate abstract ideas that are difficult to articulate through verbal forms. Moreover, it means that the whole person is treated and allowed to experience themselves as "a holistic and synthesised acting, feeling, thinking being-in-the-world, rather than as separate physical and mental qualities which bear no relation to each other" (Stolz, 2015, p. 474). Being in the world also incites the notion that teaching should be in the moment and at the "juncture between self and other" (Macintyre & Buck, 2008, p. 317).

An embodied arts-based divergence

In our interactions with teachers during the data gathering process and ana-lysis of the data, we noticed that classroom teachers were using movement activities in classrooms for a range of educational purposes, sometimes employing arts-based pedagogies. In the interviews, teachers often referred to these activities as "brain breaks", or fun activities loosely connected to embodied arts-based activities. Many of these activities incorporated dancing and singing. We were curious why teachers used brain breaks as we observed many embodied arts-based activities labelled as such. In interviews, we asked about using arts-based embodiment and classroom practices which involved movement. The responses from the teachers were coded into four themes:

- The use of physical movement activities as a break within lessons
- Arts-based activities to support learning in another subject area
- Arts-based embodied learning planned to integrate arts forms within lessons and units
- Arts-based experiences planned with student and family involvement

We report on these themes through a collection of vignettes to highlight the similarities and differences and the reasons teachers gave for their peda-gogical choices when planning and enacting the curriculum.

The use of physical movement activities as a break within lessons

During classroom observations, we noticed teachers planned short breaks within lessons where students left their desks and did physical exercises for a short period. When we asked the teachers about these breaks, they described them as a scheduled stop in the teaching block incorporating physical movement to give students a mental break from learning activities. One classroom teacher explained how she used the "popcorn game" in her Year 2 class.

> Popcorn is a game where I will say like "popcorn", and then they [the students] have to jump on the spot. Then I will say "sugar" and then go to touch the ground, and then I will say "ball". And then they have to clap the hand of one of their mates. And then I will say, "Popcorn, ball", and then they have to repeat all those mentioned movements. I use this activity as a brain break within a lesson. They [the students] get re-energised … re-focused.
>
> (Teacher 12)

In this instance, the teacher spoke about using brain breaks at 30-minute intervals during lessons as purely physical activities to help refocus her students. The children returned to the previous activity after the brain break. Brain breaks in teaching are well-documented (Ackerman, 2018; Baker et al., 2017) with Ackerman's (2018) study on the effect of brain breaks during class for children aged between 4 and 5 years, finding they allowed for increased student engagement. Brain breaks have been shown to impact academic performance positively, with research showing they decrease boredom and are an effective intervention for behaviour issues (Fedewa et al., 2021; Lengel & Kuczala, 2010; Mavilidi et al., 2020). Although there are many studies focused on aerobic movement breaks, there are not many studies that explore the use of embodied arts-based movement embedded into the lesson to achieve academic awareness, in activities that are stimulating and provide positive learning environments for students.

Group singing and group dancing featured in another example of a break within a lesson. The teacher explained how she used singing and dancing to facilitate and assist behaviour management in the classroom.

> [We] dance as a brain break to help with their behaviour management in class. We do have students who need that regular movement break to help them with their behaviour. They really enjoy the opportunities to join in the singing and the dancing in classes that break

between their lessons. So yes, we do find that can be a very effective tool and the children absolutely love that opportunity to get up and join in and participate in singing and dancing in their classroom and having a little bit of fun with their teacher. That's not sitting at the desk and doing your work.

(Teacher 8)

Teachers reported that children enjoyed singing and dancing and were engaged during this time. However, no mention was made of a change in students' behaviour or improvement in engagement in the lesson after the brain break. Done regularly, as in this example, children are building a repertoire of songs and dances through which they develop arts practices and skills. Collectively, they are participating in a group experience which teachers value for the opportunity for all children to participate and have fun.

Arts-based activities to support learning in another subject area

In the Early Years classrooms we visited, we noticed that teachers used movement and embodiment to teach spelling, maths and phonics. In the following section, we present a collection of activities observed in classrooms where teachers used music and movement to teach content.

We do a spelling popcorn game where each child has to pop up and say the next letter. Or in maths, they have to move around and become the number line and things like that. I try to incorporate as much as I can see that students are engaged.

(Teacher 12)

Students enjoy listening to music. I do the times table songs. I have kids who cannot connect the multiplication but can skip counting numbers they could not count before. Just from these songs that we sing. They sing along in their head, and they walk around singing them. So, they're practising them, and they recall them. They just enjoy it. They enjoy the music and getting up and having a dance.

(Teacher 13)

When they were struggling to make numbers last year, [the children] actually used their bodies to make the numbers ... They lay on the ground, and they had to figure out how they were going to make the numbers with their bodies.

(Teacher 13)

We teach phonics through movement and songwriting. We look particularly at music; in the beginning, we start composing our own songs. We are bringing in language and the syllables of different words and working those out. And then how can we replace that word in a song using the same amount of words with the same amount of syllables. You know so that we might do, "I am stomping". And let's replace "stomping" with something else. How many syllables are in stomping? Let's work it out. So, there is transference between Maths and into English as well.

(Teacher 8)

In these learning opportunities incorporating embodiment into classroom activities, we can see that children use their visual, auditory, and kinaesthetic perceptions to help them engage with the curriculum by creating a space where they become active learners. In classes where the teachers used activities such as song, dance, and drama to teach content, teachers spoke of the improved engagement in the learning task where all the children in the class (some of whom teachers described as reluctant learners) participated with enthusiasm. The arts enable the development and expression of "thoughts, ideas and emotions in ways that other forms of communication simply cannot" (Roy et al., 2015). Embodied learning offers possibilities for demonstrating learning beyond text and has the potential to change classroom dynamics (Gibson & Ewing, 2020). Garrett & MacGill (2021) found possibilities like this created more inclusive classrooms where children were more willing to take risks, persist and engage in dialogue than without these activities.

We observed another teaching moment where the teacher used the picture book *Fox* (2000) by Margaret Wild as part of a visual literacy lesson in a Year 3 class to teach active listening, reading comprehension and writing skills through embodied arts-based activities. The teacher asked the children to look at the different images in the book while she read the story. She used the visual representation of the pictures of the book to help students to understand the story, situation and characters presented in the book. The children worked in groups, each picking out two consecutive images in the book to interpret through movement. The children used the drama technique of still images or freeze frames to enact the actions of the characters. They then presented their version of the story through a series of freeze frames to make meaning of the text. The teacher describes the process:

> They learn about friendship and betrayal in the story of Fox, Dog and Magpie. The children love this activity as they can act out the story and become the characters. They express the emotions of fear, sadness and happiness of the characters as they move their bodies to tell the story. Once they worked out and practised their freezeframes, the different groups presented their freezeframe in a series of rolling freezeframes to tell the story in sequence. We then look at the video, and the children see the story come alive through their actions telling the story of Fox, Dog and Magpie. The children are more engaged in the learning and remember the story, emotion and setting much better than just reading the story to them. This is also evident in their understanding and writing after the presentations.
>
> (Teacher 26)

In an activity such as this, the children use gestures as well as their whole body to extend the cognitive process to turn the abstract words of the story into a more salient experience to bring the characters, their emotions and the setting alive. Teaching in an integrated way through the embodiment of the arts is an effective way to promote active, holistic and conclusive learning engagement in the classroom. Children actively participate in arts activities, making creative decisions using multiple learning modalities to create meaning.

Arts-based embodied learning planned to integrate arts forms within lessons and units

The vignettes shared here are listed in a sequence representing a metamorphosis of intentions and connectedness between movement, the arts, children's learning and enactment of the curriculum. In each story in the collection, teachers identified a place and space for purposeful use of movement in the myriad of pedagogical choices made throughout the teaching day.

One teacher discussed a unit based on the music "*The Flight of the Bumblebee*" [Rimsky-Korsakov, 1899–1900].

> *We become the bee. The bee comes out of his hive, and by listening to the piece of music over weeks, we imagine a journey … That's my leading them on a journey. Then as an assessment piece, [the children] respond to the music in a visual art piece … they take their bee wherever it wants to go. They move their body as well, so high, low, fast, and slow. All of those comparatives that are part of the music curriculum … Music lends itself to movement in that way.*
>
> (Teacher 25)

Integrating the arts, as discussed in these examples, show that the use of embodiment to teach concepts engages students holistically, permitting them to work together in open-ended learning tasks to challenge and invite creative ways of working, experimentation, self-expression and whole-body learning opportunities (Ewing, 2020; Bamford, 2006).

Similarly, in the lesson described in the introduction, we observed the integration of arts-based embodiment where the teacher was working with a Year 2 class using music, dance and drama to explore the hatching of a caterpillar and its emergence into the outside world. To begin, the children were asked to imagine not just what it would feel like to hatch from an egg but how the tiny caterpillar might feel at this juncture in its life. In a series of small provocations, the teacher led the children through an imagined experience of metamorphosis, which acknowledged the interrelationships between the art forms. The lesson appeared carefully choreographed to sequence teacher questions, and visual and musical prompts with children's responses through movement, voice, dance and drama.

The teacher expressed a clear determination to explore the interrelatedness between arts forms in lessons stating that "all lessons involve dance, drama and music. They are not separated". (Teacher 1). Although each art form in the Australian Curriculum "involves different approaches to arts practices and critical and creative thinking, they have close relationships and are often used in interrelated ways" (ACARA, n.d., para 1). The teacher indicated a deliberate preference for integrated learning, stating that using the arts in lesson planning and embedding the arts into unit planning "creates a rhythm to the unit" (Teacher 1).

Arts-based experiences planned with student and family involvement

In our final vignette, we share the story of a Year 1 teacher who worked with students and their families in her class to enable cultural connections within arts learning. In this instance, the teacher sought to build on shared experiences and the children's personal knowledge, voice and agency by connecting curriculum content and priorities with family arts practices.

> I think our students … bring with them so much cultural knowledge, like dances, that they have been exposed to outside of school. They bring a love and pride of culture. Most drama and art last year and a bit of dance last year were all connected to indigenous dance and art somehow. Because [the children] could see the purpose, make the connection. It was a way they could access the curriculum easily.
>
> (Teacher 12)

These learning opportunities to explore and share cultures through embodiment of cultural stories created safety and opened the way for dialogue between students, families and the school. The teacher noted that "… I found that [connecting] to cultural knowledge made everything more meaningful" (Teacher 12).

This notion of using embodiment to explore culture connects children more deeply with themselves to understand the connectedness between human beings and their place in the world. Freire (1993, p. 87) noted that

> [T]he importance of the body is indisputable; the body moves, acts, rememorises the struggle for its liberation; the body, in sum, desires, points out, announces, protests, curves itself, rises, designs and remakes the world.

Discussion

Arts educators have argued the strength of the arts for young children to make sense of their worlds. The process of participating and creating in arts activities such as singing, dancing, and acting, offers a powerful way in which children can use their bodies for learning (Davies, 2003). The embodiment of the arts creates opportunities for learning as the process engages children to explore imaginative play, which plays a part in developing their cognitive abilities. Using arts-based embodiment activities in a classroom promotes full engagement in learning that is personally meaningful and challenging.

Young learners use a sophisticated range of gestures, movements, and sounds to communicate, express themselves and interact with others. Through using the arts, Wright (2003) endorsed the union between "bodily kinaesthetic understanding and thinking, feeling and doing" (p. 43). For example, music and dance provide unique insights into knowing that are not available through linguistic forms of communication (Baumann, 1997). Children make meaning of the world around them using signs such as forms, shapes and gestures as modes of representation (Barton, 2015; Ewing, 2010). In our classroom observations, we saw students participating in embodied movement using these signs to respond to dance, drama and music to co-construct a shared experience. These children expressed their imagined experience of becoming a character through thinking, feeling and doing. In the learning moments, we saw arts-based embodiment come into being as body and mind became the vehicle to express their learning.

Conclusion

Our research presented in this chapter suggests that introducing and using embodiment through arts-based learning into Early Years classrooms is a tangled process. The vignettes identified a diverse range of responses that point to the complexity of incorporating arts-based embodiment in primary school classrooms. However, the significance of the transformational effect of embodied arts-based practices cannot be underestimated. Children actively interact with their surroundings through visual, auditory, kinaesthetic, emotional and other perceptions. The vignettes showed the diversity of ways that teachers incorporated and planned for movement and embodied learning in their classrooms. What stands out for us is witnessing teachers embracing the notion of embodied and stepping into the realm where the arts provide a space for self-expression, creativity, collaboration and ownership. Importantly, these opportunities can provide new avenues and variations for learning activities, increase student participation, and ignite positive engagement in learning. The assemblage of creative arts-based embodiment engagement offers an alternative way to enable teachers to consciously make decisions that enrich all children's learning experiences.

References

Ackerman, A. L. (2018). *Relationship between movement and student behaviors*. Master's Theses & Capstone Projects. Northwester College Iowa. https://nwcommons.nwciowa.edu/cgi/viewcontent.cgi?article=1108&context=education_masters

Australian Curriculum and Assessment and Reporting Authority (ACARA) (n.d.). *The Arts: F–10 Curriculum*. www.australiancurriculum.edu.au/f-10-curriculum/the-arts/

Ayala, N. A. R., Mendívil, E. G., Salinas, P., & Rios, H. (2013). Kinesthetic learning applied to mathematics using kinect. *Procedia Computer Science, 25*, 131–135.

Baker, E. A., Elliott, M., Barnidge, E., Estlund, A., Brownson, R. C., Milne, A., … & Hashimoto, D. (2017). Implementing and evaluating environmental and policy interventions for promoting physical activity in rural schools. *Journal of School Health, 87*(7), 538–545.

Bamford, A. (2006). *The wow factor: Global research compendium on the impact of the arts in education*. Waxmann Verlag.

Barton, G. (2015). Arts-based educational research in the early years. *International Research in Early Childhood Education, 6*(1), 62–78.

Barton, G., & Baguley, M. (2014). Learning through story: A collaborative, multimodal arts approach. *English Teaching: Practice and Critique, 13*(2), 93–112.

Baumann, H.D.L. (1997). Toward a poetics of vision, space and the body: Sign language and literary theory. In L. J. Davis (Ed.), *The Disability Studies Reader* (pp. 355–366). Routledge.

Block, B., & Kissell, J. L. (2001). The dance: Essence of embodiment. *Theoretical Medicine and Bioethics, 22*(1), 5–15.

Bresler, L. (2013). *Knowing bodies, moving minds: Towards embodied teaching and learning* (Vol. 3). Springer Science & Business Media.

Chao, K. J., Huang, H. W., Fang, W. C., & Chen, N. S. (2013). Embodied play to learn: Exploring kinect-facilitated memory performance. *British Journal of Educational Technology, 44*, 5.

Chomske, N. (1995). *Syntactic Structures*. Mouton.

Davies M. (2003). *Movement and dance in early childhood* (2nd ed.). Paul Chapman Publishing.

Dewey, J. (1934). *Art as experience*. Penguin Books Ltd.

Donnelly, J. E., & Lambourne, K. (2011). Classroom-based physical activity, cognition, and academic achievement. *Preventive Medicine, 52*, 36–42.

Eisner, E. W. (2002). *The arts and the creation of mind*. Yale University Press.

Enriquez, G. (2015). Reader response and embodied performance: Body-poems as performative response and performativity. In G. Enriquez, E. Johnson, S. Kontovourki, & C. A. Mallozzi (Eds.), *Literacies, learning, and the body* (pp. 57–72). Routledge.

Ewing, R. (2010). *The arts and Australian education: Realising potential*. ACER Press.

Ewing, R. (2020). Integrating the creative arts with integrity. In R. Gibson & R. Ewing, *Transforming the curriculum through the Arts*. Springer. https://doi.org/10.1007/978-3-030-52797-6_4

Fedewa, A. L., Erwin, H., Ahn, S., & Alawadi, S. (2021). The effects of desk cycles in elementary children's classroom physical activity: A feasibility study. *Journal of Occupational Therapy, Schools & Early Intervention*, 1–13. doi: 10.1080/19411243.2021.1910608

Fodor, J. (2006). How the mind works: What we still don't know. *Daedalus 135*, 86–94. https://doi.org/10.2307/20028056

Fodor, J. A. (1983). *Modularity of mind: An essay on faculty psychology*. MIT Press.

Freire, P. (1993). *Pedagogy of the city*. Continuum.

Gardner, H. (1993). *Frames of the mind: The theory of multiple intelligences 10th Anniversary Edition*. Basic Books.

Garrett, R. & MacGill, B. (2021). Fostering inclusion in school through creative and body-based learning. *International Journal of Inclusive Education, 25*(11), 1221–1235. https://doi.org/10.1080/13603116.2019.1606349

Gibson, R., & Ewing, R. (2020). *Transforming the curriculum through the arts*. Springer International Publishing.

Greene, M. (1995). *Releasing the imagination: Essays on education, the arts, and social change*. Jossey-Bass.

Greene, M. (2001). *Variations on a blue guitar: The Lincoln Center Institute lectures on aesthetic education*. Teachers College Press.

Kosmas, P., Ioannou, A., & Retalis, S. (2018). Moving bodies to moving minds: A study of the use of motion-based games in special education. *TechTrends, 62*(6), 594–601.

Kosmas, P., Ioannou, A., & Zaphiris, P. (2019). Implementing embodied learning in the classroom: Effects on children's memory and language skills. *Educational Media International, 56*(1), 59–74.

Lengel, T., & Kuczala, M. (2010). *The kinesthetic classroom: Teaching and learning through movement*. Corwin Press.

Macedonia, M. (2014). Bringing back the body into the mind: Gestures enhance word learning in foreign language. *Frontiers in Psychology, 5*, 1467.

Macedonia, M. (2019). Embodied learning: Why at school the mind needs the body. *Frontiers in Psychology, 10*. https://doi.org/10.3389/fpsyg.2019.02098

Macintyre Latta, M., & Buck, G. (2008). Enfleshing embodiment: "Falling into trust" with the body's role in teaching and learning. *Educational Philosophy and Theory, 40*(2), 315–329.

Mavilidi, M. F., Drew, R., Morgan, P. J., Lubans, D. R., Schmidt, M., & Riley, N. (2020). Effects of different types of classroom physical activity breaks on children's on-task behaviour, academic achievement and cognition. *Acta paediatrica, 109*(1), 158–165.

Merleau-Ponty, M. (1964). *Signs*. Transl. ed R. C. McCleary. Northwestern University Press.

Merleau-Ponty, M. (2012). *The phenomenology of perception*. Transl. ed D. A. Landes. Routledge.

Mueller, F. F., Edge, D., Vetere, F., Gibbs, M. R., Agamanolis, S., Bongers, B., & Sheridan, J. G. (2011, May 7). *Designing sports: A framework for exertion games* [Paper presentation]. SIGCHI Conference on Human Factors in Computing Systems.

Nguyen, D. J., & Larson, J. B. (2015). Don't forget about the body: Exploring the curricular possibilities of embodied pedagogy. *Innovative Higher Education, 40*(4), 331–344. https://doi.org/10.1007/s10755-015-9319-6

O'Toole, J. (2012). Art, creativity, and motivation. In C. Sinclair, N. Jeanneret, N & J. O'Toole (Eds.), *Education in the arts* (2nd ed.) (pp. 7–14). Oxford University Press.

Piaget, J. (1951). *Play, dreams and imitation in childhood*. Routledge.

Rankin, J., Garrett, R., & MacGill, B. (2021). Critical encounters: Enacting social justice through creative and body-based learning. *The Australian Educational Researcher, 48*, 281–302. https://doi.org/10.1007/s13384-020-00389-6

Rigney, L., Garrett, R., Curry, M., & MacGill, B. (2020). Culturally responsive pedagogy and mathematics through creative and body-based learning: Urban Aboriginal schooling. *Education and Urban Society, 52*(8), 1159–1180. https://doi.org/10.1177/0013124519896861

Roy, D., Baker, W., & Hamilton, A. (2015). *Teaching the Arts: Early childhood and primary education* (2nd ed.). Cambridge University Press.

Shin, J. K. (2017). Get up and sing! Get up and move! Using songs and movement with young learners of English. *English Teaching Forum, 55*(2), 14–25.

Shor, I. & Freire, P. (1987). *A pedagogy for liberation*. Bergin and Garvey.

Soylu, F., Lester, F. K., and Newman, S. D. (2018). You can count on your fingers: the role of fingers in early mathematical development. *Journal of Numerical Cognition, 4*, 107–135.https://doi.org/10.5964/jnc.v4i1.85

Stolz, S. A. (2015). Embodied learning. *Educational Philosophy and Theory, 47*(5), 474–487. https://doi.org/10.1080/00131857.2013.879694

Vaesen, K. (2014). Dewey on extended cognition and epistemology. *Philosophical Issues, 24*, 426–438.

Whitmore, K. F. (2015). "Becoming the story" in the joyful world of Jack and the Beanstalk. *Language Arts, 93*(1), 25–37.

Wild, M. (2000). *Fox*. Allen & Unwin.

Wright, S. (2003). *The arts, young children and learning*. Pearson Education.

The body as an instrument of knowing

Kinaesthetic learning with and through the arts

Susan Chapman

Introduction

The aims of this chapter are to present a theoretical position on kinaesthetic learning in Early Childhood contexts, to provide new knowledge by demonstrating the capacity of an innovative Arts Immersion approach to address children's kinaesthetic needs, and then to illustrate this with examples from teaching and research. The chapter will consider developmental changes regarding kinaesthetic experiences between birth and eight years of age; debate around the concepts of kinaesthetic learning as a learning style and as one of Gardner's (1983) multiple intelligences; the epistemology of kinaesthetic learning – the opposing perspectives of mind versus body dualism and mind-body as one cohesive entity; and connections between kinaesthetic, embodied and somatic knowing. The chapter then explores the relationship between an Arts Immersion pedagogy and kinaesthetic learning – highlighting teaching strategies which contribute to brain development in young children, and suggests the final implications for challenging established teaching practices and supporting kinaesthetic learning through arts subjects. These sections begin by painting a picture of a baby's early kinaesthetic experiences.

DOI: 10.4324/9781003268772-7

Children entering the world

From birth, children are sentient beings, growing their perceptions of themselves and the world through their experience of feelings and sensations. Their senses are alive to the adventure of inhabiting an embodied identity. For young children, their bodily exploration of their surroundings builds a growing awareness of what it means to be in the world. A baby watches with fascination as their fingers move, silhouetted against the light; they slap a surface or shake a filled container to make a sound; they smell the people who cuddle them and feel the movement to music as they are held; they experiment making their own sounds, copying the mouth shapes of faces they can touch as they hold a conversation without words; they kick and roll, flap and crawl; they feel the smoothness of mango skin and the roughness of tree bark; and they taste flavours and textures as their sensory capacities expand. The early childhood years from birth to age 8 are a rich time of rapid growth and formation as children develop their own agency by increasingly having their own ideas, attitudes and opinions. These are manifested in embodied expressions of understanding which emerge from kinaesthetic experiences that are physical and tactile in nature.

Terms about physical and tactile experiences

There are several terms used in discussions regarding kinaesthetic learning, each demonstrating some aspects of shared understanding and difference. The term, kinaesthetic learning, has been described broadly as "physically engaging classroom exercises" (Begel et al., 2004, p. 183) and more specifically as "muscular movement in response to visual, auditory, and tactile stimulation" (Grant, 1985, p. 455). What these descriptions have in common is the idea that kinaesthetic learning involves an awareness of the body actively participating in physical and tactile experiences. Debate has ensued regarding the extent to which kinaesthetic learning remains relevant to all children as they grow older, or whether this relevance is reduced to becoming a preferred style of learning for a specific group of learners.

Is kinaesthetic learning a learning style?

The theory that kinaesthetic learning is a Learning Style (LS) is based on the 'matching' hypothesis which contends that matching instruction with LS could improve student learning. However, this idea has been consistently critiqued over time and found wanting. At the end of the twentieth century, Reynolds (1997) argued that criticism of the LS theory (and the earlier term, cognitive styles) began in the 1970s, emanating from within cognitive psychology and from educators who expressed concern that this theory encouraged decontextualised learning leading to the risk of reinforcing social prejudice. Despite literature reporting its lack of validity, research evidence shows no decline in the continued widespread support for the LS theory (Newton, 2015; Newton & Miah, 2017; Newton & Salvi, 2020). In Newton and Salavi's (2020) systematic review, covering 37 studies from 18 countries between 2009 and 2020, educators' self-reported belief, use, and planned use of the LS matching hypothesis was high. For instance, "95.4% of trainee (pre-service) teachers agreed that matching instructions to Learning Styles is effective" (Newton & Salvi, 2020, p. 1). However, supporting educators to develop critical thinking skills contributed to a subsequent 37% average decline in self-reported belief in LS theory (Newton & Salvi, 2020). Teacher educators have a key role to play in encouraging pre-service teachers to critique the theory of LS by examining academic literature.

Substantial academic criticism of LS theory by psychologists and educators argues that this theory is an unsubstantiated "myth" (Brown & Kaminske, 2018; Newton, 2015; Newton & Miah, 2017; Newton & Salvi, 2020; Reiner & Willingham, 2010). Psychologists, Reiner and Willingham (2010) point out that students differ in their capacity to learn, their genetic makeup, their interests and their background knowledge, which is a much broader purview than the concept of a preferred learning style. These authors discredit the categorisation of learning into 'styles' described as visual, auditory or kinaesthetic, by referring to research in which students in controlled conditions demonstrated equivalent learning regardless of their preferred mode ('style') of learning. They contend that belief in Learning Styles persists because of a failure to perceive the critical differences between styles and abilities; the notion that Learning Styles represent an egalitarian view of education, and confirmation bias in which this theory is viewed as "common knowledge." A central consideration in this debate should be that since all humans have a body, kinaesthetic experiences are a given rather than a choice because the body is essential for human existence. An alternative theory is to distinguish between the role of kinaesthetic learning in teaching pedagogy and the theory of kinaesthetic intelligence.

Bodily-kinaesthetic intelligence and multiple intelligences

In some instances, Howard Gardner's theory of Multiple Intelligences (MI) has been described as a subset of the LS hypothesis (Gudnason, 2017). However, Gardner has disagreed with this description, explaining that Learning Styles represent different approaches to learning and teaching, while intelligences refer to the ways in which we use our brains (Gardner, 1993; Gudnason, 2017). In 1983, Gardner proposed several types of intelligence including bodily-kinaesthetic intelligence which could be identifiable as a "liking for hands-on and practical learning situations; aptitude for dancing, gymnastics and all kinds of physical sports; (and) a tendency to use gestures and respond to tactile surfaces" (Dinham & Chalk, 2018, p. 36). Research has been conducted in Early Childhood settings where kinaesthetic learning has been positioned as one of Gardner's multiple intelligences (bodily-kinaesthetic intelligence) to: develop literacy skills in kindergarten children because of its physical and tactile approach (Curtis, 2019); analyse kinaesthetic intelligence as one of five components of brain-based teaching in kindergarten (Das, 2018); investigate the impact of hopscotch towards the growth of kinaesthetic intelligence in three–four-year-old children (Laely & Yudi, 2018); use a game model based on a cultural values approach in developing interpersonal and kinaesthetic intelligences in young children (Hanafiah, Nurapriani, Gaffar, 2018); and learn through movement activities and traditional songs to enhance kinaesthetic intelligence in children aged five–six years (Yetti & Muanivah, 2017). There are a range of responses to Gardner's MI theory, all varying in their degree of support and negative critique. Shearer and Karanian (2017) report neuroscientific evidence supporting Gardner's hypothesis that measurements of general intelligence tend to align with linguistic and logical-mathematical intelligences and state that "there is robust evidence that each intelligence possesses neural coherence that is clear, distinct and aligned with accepted cognitive-neural correlates" (p. 211). Gardner and Moran (2006) have responded to Waterhouse's (2006) critique that MI theory lacks validating data by contending that critics sought to oversimplify Multiple Intelligence theory, thereby failing to realise that Gardner never intended for his work to represent "'the' definitive description of human cognitive capacities, (but) (r)ather... that relatively independent yet interacting intelligences provide a better understanding of the variety and scope of human cognitive feats than do competing accounts" (p. 227). Whether subscribing to Gardner's theory or not, the notion of a diverse range of cognitive processes provides food for thought, challenging the concept of intelligence as a single homogenous entity, particularly when considering different ways of knowing.

An epistemology of kinaesthetic learning

Considering the epistemological underpinnings of kinaesthetic learning invites educators to explore the process of how children come to know. Is it that children learn primarily with their body or their mind, through body and mind as separate processes, initially through the body but progressively through the mind as they get older, through whichever means of knowing they prefer, or continually through body and mind in an inextricable connection? Alexander (2017) speaks of kinaesthetic knowing which relies on physical exchanges that are associated with feeling, sensation, impulse, instinct and gesture to produce "reliable knowledge without recourse to language, concepts, propositions, or representations" (p. 8). This explanation, while highly valuing bodily knowing, appears to view body and mind as two independent ways of knowing, and suggests that language is assumed to be verbal. A health professional viewpoint may favour a more biologically-based explanation for kinaesthetic learning in which the proprioceptive system depends on sensory receptors, located in muscles, joints and tendons, to send detailed messages to the brain in order to regulate sensory processing in the body. The two contrasting practice traditions which follow represent opposing views of the relationship between body and mind: the first, positioning the mind as vastly superior to the body in terms of learning; and the second, positioning body and mind as co-equal inseparable partners in knowing.

The dualism of mind versus body

Much of the literature which focuses on kinaesthetic learning criticises the partitioning of mind and body that has emanated from Western rationalism and been embedded in the education systems that have grown out of this philosophy. The dualism segregating mind and body has been historically attributed to Plato (Peters, 2004) and continued by Descartes in his famous statement, "Cogito ergo sum: I think therefore I am" (Descartes, 1968, p. 53). There is agreement that Western scientific processes have supported this separation, giving rise to deeply privileging the mind over the body (Babour, 2004; Buono, 2019; Ellingson, 2008; Juntunen & Hyvonen, 2004). This chapter argues that the separation of body and mind does not accurately represent the complexity of kinaesthetic learning experiences for young children, or for any age group. In literature critiquing this dualism, a line of philosophical thought has emerged, contending not only that mind and body should not be separated, but that is indeed impossible to do so.

Merleau-Ponty: a mind-body philosophy

The French phenomenological philosopher Maurice Merleau-Ponty explains the inextricable connection of mind and body in terms of the subjective perceptions of body interacting with the external world. In considering individual experience, he points to our essential embodied experience of the world in which "our body is not an object for an 'I think', it is a grouping of lived-through meanings which moves towards equilibrium" (Merleau-Ponty, 1962, p. 153). To Merleau-Ponty, the embodied nature of human existence centres on the lived body which Paparo (2011) describes as "the living, breathing, acting and thinking self" (p. 23). From this viewpoint, our lived experience necessarily precedes the abstraction required in analysis and reflection because our body perception, or embodied knowing, is the means through which we learn to understand the world (Merleau-Ponty, 1962). Barbour (2004) advocates for restoring the value of lived experience where knowledge is co-constructed at an individual and collective level rather than received as a generic product formed of rational argument. She contends that mental activity should not be privileged over our lived experience in which relationships with the world are formed. In fact, the process of understanding is shared by the thinking body and the acting mind. When body and mind share in the development of understanding, cognition can be an enacted rather than exclusively internal process. Drawing on Merleau-Ponty's philosophy, Peters (2004) explains cognition as enactive and embodied while considering knowing to be inseparable from action. Merleau-Ponty's philosophy holds true especially for young children, for whom there is no separation between body and mind. They develop embodied perceptions, experiencing the world through their senses and through physical and tactile sensations. This is the perspective that young children bring when they participate in more formal learning situations.

Children entering formal learning settings

Most students enter formal learning settings with a sense of play, ready to discover more of the world. For them, play naturally provides kinaesthetic learning which builds embodied knowing since the body remembers learning through the senses and through physical action. Matthews (1998) describes play as "the personal embodiment of one's imagination, the ability to transform oneself into what one wants to become" (p. 238). In the early years of formal schooling, children still need embodied experiences through which they can further the exploration of their surroundings, themselves and others through their lived experiences, senses, and the sensations of tactile experiences. Dinham and Chalk (2018) describe five types of play, each involving kinaesthetic learning derived from embodied knowing: imaginative and socio-dramatic play; constructive and investigative play; explorative play; directed and scaffolded play; and sensory play. They explain that during this time children in Early Childhood (EC) learning contexts need opportunities for embodied lived experiences to: "develop their visual, aural and tactile discernment; strengthen their muscles; refine their motor skills, hand-eye coordination, control and spatial judgement; improve balance and poise; and build endurance" (p. 66). Yetti and Muanivah (2017) point out that during EC, children have a high sensitivity to tactile and sensory forms of stimulation in their environment. They suggest that educators have an important role in providing opportunities for kinaesthetic learning experiences which correspond to the stages of early childhood development. In doing so, they regard the physical development of children as part of kinaesthetic intelligence in accordance with Gardner's Multiple Intelligences (1983). Friedberg (2020) highlights the fact that children are essentially "movers" who cumulatively develop motor skills in a particular order, although not at the same rate. Through physical activity and movement, they develop independence, a sense of self, social-emotional skills, overall health and growth as well as "strength, stamina, balance and coordination" (Friedberg, 2020, p. 111). When knowing is an embodied experience, separating the terms mind and body requires re-examination.

Connecting kinaesthetic, embodied and somatic knowing

Viewing the mind and body together in an interdependent relationship is more clearly represented by using the amalgamated term, mind-body. To support a theoretical position on mind-body, consideration will be given to the epistemological connections between kinaesthetic knowing (previously discussed), embodied knowing (sometimes referred to as embodied cognition) and somatic knowing. Embodied knowing has been described as knowledge that resides in the body and is gained through the body (Nagatomo, 1992), and as a sensory experience of the lived body in which the body is a knowing-subject (Ellingson, 2008; Tanaka, 2011). Our bodies are essential for organising ourselves in our environment as they communicate what we know, how we feel, and how we can be and become in the world (Coetzee, 2018). This understanding aligns well with Australia's Early Years Learning Framework which outlines the three foundational concepts of belonging, being and becoming to describe the process where children are linked to family, community, culture and place, as they develop relationships, identity and learn about the world around them (Department of Education Employment and Workplace Relations, 2009). This holistic view of our embodied identity and embodied experiences can be understood through the process of somatic knowing.

Somatic knowing can be described as an experiential mind-body knowing which relates to or affects the body or body-based mindfulness drawing on an awareness of internal physical perception and experience. Matthews (1998) contends that somatic knowing involves "sense, precept, and mind/body action and reaction – a knowing, feeling, and acting that includes more of the broad range of human experience than that delimited within the traditionally privileged, distanced, disembodied range of discursive conceptualization" (pp. 236–237). A similar co-equal integration of all aspects of self is reflected in Buono's (2019) recommendation of mindfully somatic pedagogy to support young children's first-person bodily experiences in interdisciplinary contexts. With their focus on holistic lived experiences, somatic, embodied and kinaesthetic knowing are at the heart of the arts and applied culture. They provide an epistemological connection to the arts-based pedagogy of Arts Immersion which pushes back against the separation of mind and body.

The arts and kinaesthetic learning

Young children are drawn to the arts and play to learn and to communicate what they have come to know. According to Wright (2012), the arts provide an enactive mode of representing the world, called artistic knowing, which blends "thought, emotion and action" (p. 4) to portray or depict ideas, stories or emotions. Artistic knowing therefore shares the same mind-body approach as kinaesthetic, embodied and somatic knowing, drawing on cultural, social and individual influences. The mind-body is partly culturally constructed but further shaped (enabled or restricted) by our diverse individual histories (Barbour, 2004), which the arts can both reflect and influence through individual and collective creativity. Wright (2012) contends that young children's flexibility in manipulating symbol systems is well supported through the arts due to a capacity for expressing and communicating the richest aspects of human existence. However, she warns that educators have a window of opportunity to build on children's imaginative ingenuity during EC years which can set the trajectory for children's future development. These mind-body opportunities for kinaesthetic arts-based learning invite broader understandings of language beyond word-based symbols. Arts-based languages hold rich potential for developing pedagogical approaches which support kinaesthetic learning.

Arts Immersion

The Arts Immersion pedagogical approach developed by Chapman (2015) uses the unique arts languages as domains of learning and as vehicles to access other learning areas. Eisner (2005) describes language as "the use of any form of representation in which meaning is conveyed or construed" (p. 342). The arts subjects of dance, drama, media arts, music and visual art function as languages providing "a sense of home and a mother language for many, producing their own unique semiotic systems which give rise to unique expressions and a range of literacies" (Chapman & O'Gorman, 2022, p. 37). Findings from an action research case study in a primary school using an Arts Immersion approach to learning suggest that improved student outcomes included: enhanced engagement with learning; improved focus and knowledge retention; more equitable opportunities for learning; increased levels of social-emotional wellbeing; and evidence of deeper cognition. In kinaesthetic learning, meaning is represented through an awareness of the body actively participating in physical and tactile experiences. Through the languages of the arts, the body becomes an instrument of knowing, a crucial means to unite the mind-body in the service of embodied knowing. This view is also reflected in Wright's (2012) position where she describes the arts languages as supraverbal, noting that "(b)ecause all of the arts involve motor responses and the senses, our perception, awareness, judgement and the expression of ideas encompass 'special' ways of knowing that are quite different from linguistic or scientific ways" (p. 7). These mind-body connections formed through physical and tactile experiences in the arts provide fertile grounds for kinaesthetic learning.

Meaningful mind-body learning experiences foster brain development in young children. Arts-based mind-body experiences can support the conditions identified by neuroscientists as important for natural brain development in EC. The strategies outlined in Table 7.1 have been taught to pre-service EC teachers (Chapman & O'Gorman, 2022) and used in Arts Immersion research in a primary school (Chapman, 2018).

Arts literacy from inclusive kinaesthetic learning

Since language is the vehicle for developing literacy, broader understandings of language will be mirrored in more inclusive forms of literacy. The capacity of the arts to move beyond word-based text allows for kinaesthetic forms of language to be used by children for meaning-making. Facility and competence in expressing understanding and emotions through arts languages can therefore contribute to more inclusive definitions of literacy, of which kinaesthetic literacy is one component. The following definitions of arts literacy reveal the inclusion of a kinaesthetic dimension: Arts literacy "encompasses the integration of body, mind, and soul through musical, spatial, bodily kinaesthetic and other aspects of artistic expression" (Wright, 2003, p. 29); and, arts literacy is "interpretive and expressive fluency through symbolic form, whether aural/sonic, embodied, textual, visual, written or a combination of these within the context of a particular art form" (Barton, 2014, p. 3). These definitions highlight the multimodal nature of the arts and the potential for mind-body experiences.

Table 7.1 Creating positive learning environments through kinaesthetic learning in the arts

Creating an active, stimulating learning environment based on findings from neuroscience (Rushton, Juola-Rushton, & Larkin, 2009, p. 360)	Kinaesthetic learning supported through the arts
The physical learning environment is non-threatening yet stimulating.	Rotating use of props and costumes for dramatic play; students' and others' artworks are displayed; music played to calm or energise children; variety of musical instruments, visual art materials and media arts devices available for safe student use; flexible learning space facilitates student movement
Large blocks of time are made available for exploration.	Process drama – students and teacher working in and out of role collaborating to create an imaginary world; improvising music to go with a short dramatic presentation to reflect mood/ emotion for image/story; use variety of drama strategies to encourage inferential thinking and draw children into literature; creating class mural/ media artwork for Harmony Day, or themed posters on a theme (e.g. kindness, courage, helpfulness)
Children have choice over what they engage with and are viewed as the "expert."	Choose a stimulus (painting, photo, object, sound, music) to develop an arts product, process or performance; use drama strategy of Mantle of the Expert - children assume role of experts (e.g. expert authors, illustrators), teacher is author who doesn't know how to finish their story (Ewing & Saunders, 2016)

(*continued*)

Table 7.1 Cont.

Creating an active, stimulating learning environment based on findings from neuroscience (Rushton, Juola-Rushton, & Larkin, 2009, p. 360)	Kinaesthetic learning supported through the arts
Hands-on, experiential learning is the norm, not the isolated lesson, and children have real events to explore, read and write about.	Singing and dancing for celebrations to represent different cultures; making musical instruments – STEAM activity; acting in role as people from an earlier historical time; creating their own radio programme with sound effects
Lessons are modelled for the children and ample opportunities are provided to explore, play, and celebrate.	Teacher demonstrates how to play an instrument, sing a song, use a visual art or media arts technique, take on the role of another character; use gradual release of responsibility; students explore ideas individually and in collaboration with their peers, engage in creative play, and celebrate their outcomes by sharing them with each other or another class (performance/exhibition)
Literature response activities connect to the child's real world.	Children's literature unpacked by using drama strategies such as postcard, conscience alley, freeze frames, role on the wall, hot seat, visualisation, soundscape, mime, role play, role walk (Ewing & Saunders; 2016)
Open dialogue takes place between the students and the teacher and among students.	Teacher and students share collaborative creative problem-solving and critical thinking to make or respond to artworks
Curriculum across all content areas is integrated, and opportunities for meaningful problem-solving are provided.	Use the arts languages to access learning across all content areas; creating a "living sustainably" dance; use Teacher in Role (drama) to solve mathematical problems

Table 7.1 Cont.

Creating an active, stimulating learning environment based on findings from neuroscience (Rushton, Juola-Rushton, & Larkin, 2009, p. 360)	Kinaesthetic learning supported through the arts
Assessment strategies are an authentic outgrowth of children's activities, and lead to a sense of accomplishment rather than stress.	Minibeast persuasive text performance: in pairs students take on the mimed role of a minibeast (e.g. ant, spider, snail) and their publicity manager who explains why this is the best minibeast in the world while minibeast mimes the points mentioned

This is particularly important for young children as they easily move across modes using cross-modal symbols, metaphors, and analogy to make meaning because their current vocabulary isn't sufficient for the task (Dinham, 2020; Wright, 2012). For instance, a box can become a car, and a space can become another planet. Children enact stories and kinaesthetically explore ideas with sensory- and emotion-based language (Dinham, 2020; Wright, 2012). They can use physical spatial metaphors in music to describe the shape of a melody or the texture of a song, and they can move in a certain way to show whether they are a lion or a robot. Through the languages of the arts, young children can inhabit the kinaesthetic metaphors they create to make meaning.

Final implications

Challenging established teaching practices

Unfortunately, many of the embodied approaches for kinaesthetic learning outlined in this chapter are often ignored or trivialised in formal learning settings in favour of narrow pedagogies privileging passive sedentary learning dominated by word-based text. The push for data in schools and demand for teacher accountability in assuring students reach required benchmarks in national testing programmes appears in some cases to be eroding more creative and inclusive pedagogical approaches to learning and teaching. Multiliteracies that are derived from multimodal ways of thinking and learning are needed to address resistance to mind-body teaching practices (Wright, 2012). The arts have an important role in challenging the removal of kinaesthetic learning from EC contexts.

Kinaesthetic learning manifested in arts subjects

The arts provide meaning-making experiences that naturally involve kinaesthetic learning. The mind-body becomes an integrated instrument of expression and knowing for the purpose of meaning-making. Dance and music provide opportunities for moving to music to increase sensory input, build physical fitness, develop social-emotional skills, enhance imaginative creativity and bring joy (Friedberg, 2020). Young children can explore: whole body movements, spatial dimensions, moving body parts, singing songs with body percussion, the sounds of simple percussion instruments, using music and dance for transitions in the daily schedule, interpretation through movement, songs to develop gross motor and fine motor skills, moving to musical rhythms, clapping to songs, dancing and music-making individually and with others, and improvising and remembering musical or dance patterns to create and perform music or dance pieces (Dinham & Chalk, 2018; Friedberg, 2020). Drama provides opportunities for children to embody the perspective of other characters and roles in other times and situations. They do this based on the concept of metaxis in which they can simultaneously inhabit the reality of their own world and the reality of a created world through the willing suspension of disbelief (Ewing & Saunders, 2016). The kinaesthetic experience of taking on another role (human or non-human) or engaging in imaginative play encourages empathy by developing an appreciation of other perspectives and lived experiences. Drama helps children to enact their story through kinaesthetic means, using a mind-body approach to knowing and thinking deeply. In visual art, children engage with the tactile experience of experimenting with a range of materials, using different colours and textures to create 2D and 3D artworks and exploring a variety of approaches to make meaning as they develop fine and gross motor skills (Dinham & Chalk, 2018; Wright, 2018). Through media arts, children can combine the experiences of the other arts subjects using digital platforms for meaning-making. Each arts subject can manifest kinaesthetic learning that is developmentally appropriate for a range of EC contexts.

Conclusion

As sentient beings who are primed to explore the world through physical and tactile experiences, young children need kinaesthetic learning experiences for their healthy development. Research does not support the view that kinaesthetic learning is a style of learning but does provide neuroscientific evidence to support the benefits of kinaesthetic learning and the notion of Gardner's kinaesthetic intelligence. Evidence from research regarding an Arts Immersion approach in a primary school setting suggests that there are a range of positive student outcomes derived from this arts-based pedagogy which draws on kinaesthetic learning. This new knowledge positions arts languages as broader, more inclusive options to word-based language, which can support brain development in young children. By taking advantage of a window of opportunity in EC where children hold great potential for imaginative ingenuity, arts-based kinaesthetic learning can establish an expansive and inclusive learning trajectory. Key researchers in the field continue to report the value of arts-based pedagogy in accessing kinaesthetic learning to benefit young children.

Traditional approaches to learning have tended to separate mind and body, privileging the mind as a superior form of knowing and positioning the body as an inferior accessory. Such views have crept into EC contexts where children may be denied the opportunity of mind-body learning in the cause of raising test scores. However, there are important gains for young children in replacing the dualism of mind versus body with more inclusive pedagogical approaches based on Merleau-Ponty's idea of the interconnected mind-body. Further research is required to ascertain the extent to which arts-based kinaesthetic learning strategies are understood by EC pre-service teachers and implemented by teachers in EC contexts. Research projects considering the comparative benefits for children experiencing an arts-based kinaesthetic learning approach and those experiencing a more traditional approach would provide valuable data for discussion. The theoretical underpinnings in this chapter challenge the prevailing idea in some EC settings that kinaesthetic learning and arts pedagogy represent inferior forms of knowledge acquisition and brain development. This chapter does not claim to present conclusive evidence regarding the benefits of an Arts Immersion in EC contexts, as the case study involved older children in one primary school. However, arts-based research consistently reveals benefits for children of all ages. The key purpose of this chapter is to provoke deeper thought into justifying the benefits of kinaesthetic learning through the notion of the mind-body. The arts have a key role to play in this process, especially through the concept of Arts Immersion, where the unique arts languages reflect mind-body understanding and foster the embodied and somatic knowing found in kinaesthetic learning. For the body to become an instrument of knowing, the mind-body must act as an agent of meaning-making.

References

Alexander, Z. C. (2017) *Kinaesthetic knowing: Aesthetics, epistemology, modern design*. The University of Chicago Press.

Barbour, K. (2004). Embodied ways of knowing. *Waikato Journal of Education, 10,* 227–238.

Barton, G. (2014). Literacy and the arts: Interpretation and expression of symbolic form. In G. Barton (Ed.), *Literacy in the arts: Retheorising learning and teaching* (pp. 3–19). Springer.

Begel, A., Garcia, D. D., & Wolfman, S. A. (2004). Kinesthetic learning in the classroom, in *SIGCSE Bulletin (Association for Computing Machinery, Special Interest Group on Computer Science Education)*. [Online]. 36(1), 183–184.

Brown, A. M., & Kaminske, A. N. (2018). *Five teaching and learning myths – debunked: A guide for teachers*. Routledge.

Buono, A. (2019). Interweaving a mindfully somatic pedagogy into an early childhood classroom. *Pedagogies: An International Journal, 14*(2), 150–168. https://doi.org/10.1080/155448OX.2019.1597723

Chapman, S. N. (2015). Arts Immersion: Using the arts as a language across the primary school curriculum. *Australian Journal of Teacher Education, 40*(9), 86–101. http://dx.doi.org/10.14221/ajte.2015v40n9.5

Chapman, S. N. (2018). *Arts Immersion across the curriculum: An action research case study in using the Arts as the home language in a primary school classroom.* (Doctoral Dissertation, Griffith University, Brisbane, Australia). http://hdl.handle.net/10072/384903

Chapman, S. N., & O'Gorman, L. (2022). Transforming learning environments in early childhood contexts through the arts: Responding to the United Nations sustainable development goals. *International Journal of Early Childhood, 54*(1), 33–50. https://doi.org/10.1007/s13158-022-00320-3

Coetzee, M.-H. (2018). Embodied knowledge(s), embodied pedagogies and performance. *South African Theatre Journal, 31*(1), 1–4. https://doi.org/10.1080/10137548.2018.1425527

Curtis, K. C. (2019) *Teacher perceptions of kinesthetic learning during literacy instruction*. ProQuest Dissertations Publishing. 13810546.

Das, S. W. H. (2018, July). The character education of early childhood: Brain-based teaching approach. In *2018–3rd International Conference on Education, Sports, Arts and Management Engineering (ICESAME 2018)* (pp. 25–28). Atlantis Press.

Department of Education Employment and Workplace Relations. (2009). *Early years learning framework*. www.acecqa.gov.au/sites/default/files/201802/belonging_being_and_becoming_the_early_years_learning_framework_for_australia.pdf

Descartes, R. (1968). *Discourse on method and the meditations*. (F. E. Sutcliffe, Trans.). Penguin Books. (Original work published 1637).

Dinham, J. (2020). *Delivering authentic arts education, 4th ed*. Cengage Learning.

Dinham, J., & Chalk, B. (2018). *It's arts play: Young children belonging, being and becoming through the arts*. Oxford University Press.

Eisner, E. (2005). Opening a shuttered window: An introduction to a special section on the arts and the intellect. *The Phi Delta Kappan, 87*(1), 8–10. doi:10.1177/003172170508700104

Ellingson, L. L. (2008). Embodied knowledge. In L. M. Given (Ed.), *The SAGE Encyclopedia of Qualitative Research Methods* (pp. 44–245). Sage.

Ewing, R., & Saunders, N. A. (2016). *The school drama book: Drama, literature and literacy in the creative classroom*. Currency Press.

Friedberg, J. (2020). *Music with babies and young children: Activities to encourage bonding, communication and wellbeing*. Jessica Kingsley Publishers.

Gardner, H. (1993). *Multiple intelligences: The theory in practice*. Basic Books.

Gardner, H., & Moran, S. (2006). The science of multiple intelligences theory: A response to Lynn Waterhouse. *Educational Psychologist, 41*(4), 227–232. https://doi.org/10.1207/s15326985ep4104_2

Grant, S. M. (1985). The kinesthetic approach to teaching: Building a foundation for learning. *Journal of Learning Disabilities, 18*(8), 455–462. https://doi.org/10.1177/002221948501800803

Gudnason, J. (2017). Learning styles in education: A critique. *BU Journal of Graduate Studies in Education, 9*(2), 19–23.

Hanafiah, H., Nurapriani, R., & Gaffar, M. A. (2018, November). Game model based on cultural values approach in developing interpersonal and kines-thetic intelligences in early childhood. In *4th International Conference on Early Childhood Education. Semarang Early Childhood Research and Education Talks* (pp. 1–7). Atlantis Press.

Juntunen, M.-L., & Hyvönen, L. (2004). Embodiment in musical knowing: How body movement facilitates learning within Dalcroze Eurhythmics. *British Journal of Music Education, 21*(2), 199–214. https://doi.org/10.1017/S0265051704005686

Laely, K., & Yudi, D. (2018). The impact of hopscotch game towards the growth of kinesthetic intelligence on 3-4 year old children. *Early Childhood Research Journal (ECRJ)*, *1*(1), 21–28.

Matthews, J. C. (1998) Somatic knowing and education. *The Educational Forum, 62*(3), 236–242. https://doi.org/10.1080/00131729808984349

Merleau-Ponty, M. (1962). (C. Smith, Trans.) *Phenomenology of perception*. The Humanities Press.

Newton, P. M. (2015). The learning styles myth is thriving in higher education. *Frontiers in Psychology, 6*(1908), 1–5.

Newton, P. M., & Miah, M. (2017). Evidence-based higher education–is the learning styles "myth" important? *Frontiers in Psychology, 8*(444), 1–9.

Newton, P. M., & Salvi, A. (2020). How common is belief in the learning styles neuromyth, and does it matter? A pragmatic systematic review. *Frontiers in education (Lausanne). [Online] 5*(602451), 1–14.

Nagatomo, S. (1992). *Attunement through the Body*. SUNY Press.

Paparo, S. A. (2011). *Embodying singing in the choral classroom: A somatic approach to teaching and learning*. ProQuest Dissertations Publishing. UMI Number: 3487534.

Peters, M. (2004). Education and the philosophy of the body: Bodies of knowledge and knowledges of body. In L. Bresler (Ed.). *Knowing bodies, moving minds: Towards embodied teaching and learning* (pp. 13–28). Springer.

Reynolds, M. (1997). Learning styles: A critique. *Management Learning, 28*(2), 115–133. https://doi.org/10.1080/00131729808984349

Riener, C., & Willingham, D. (2010). The myth of learning styles. *Change: The Magazine of Higher Learning, 42*(5), 32–35.

Rushton, S., Juola-Rushton, A., & Larkin, E. (2009). Neuroscience, play and early childhood education: Connections, implications and assessment. *Early Childhood Education Journal, 37*(5), 351–361. https://doi.org/10.1007/s10643-009-0359-3

Shearer, C. B., & Karanian, J. M. (2017). The neuroscience of intelligence: Empirical support for the theory of multiple intelligences? *Trends in Neuroscience and Education, 6*, 211–223. https://doi.org/10.1016/j.tine.2017.02.002

Tanaka, S. (2011) The notion of embodied knowledge. In P. Stenner, J. Cromby, J. Motzkau, J. Yen, & Y. Haosheng (Eds.). *Theoretical Psychology: Global transformations and challenges*, pp. 149–157. Captus Press.

Waterhouse, L. (2006). Multiple intelligences, the Mozart effect, and emotional intelligence: A critical review. *Educational Psychologist, 41*, 207–225.

Wright, S. (2003). *Children, meaning-making and the arts* (1st ed.). Pearson.

Wright, S. (2012). *Children, meaning-making and the arts* (2nd ed.). Pearson.

Wright, S. (2018). Good question: Exploring epistemology and ontology in arts education and creativity. In *Creativities in arts education, research and practice* (pp. 101–115). Brill.

Yetti, E., & Muanivah, H. (2017, January). Improved intelligence kinesthetic children ages 5–6 years through activities of motion and song. In *Proceeding abstract* (pp. 41–44), ADNI International Multidisciplinary Conference.

Digital technologies and kinaesthetic learning for Early Years boys

Georgina Barton and
Rebecca Trimble-Roles

Introduction

Evidence suggests that boys' literacy learning achievements are generally below that of their female counterparts (Alloway, Freebody, Gilbert & Muspratt, 2002). Reasons for why boys develop differently include changes in cognitive and physical development (Moss & Washbrook, 2016); contextual factors such as social and cultural background (Disenhaus, 2015); and varied interest areas and achievement goals (Alloway et al., 2002; Millard, 2002). In Australia, a national inquiry was carried out to understand why "boys were not achieving as well as girls across a broad spectrum of measures" (Fletcher, 2000). One recommendation from this inquiry suggested that schools be supported to develop boys' direct involvement in negotiating their own learning environment including the physical space. Unfortunately, some 20 years later results have minimally changed for boys.

In response to the ongoing gap between boys' and girls' literacy learning (Henry et al., 2012), we decided to implement a research project within an Early Years boys' classroom. In this chapter, we discuss how this project used kinaesthetic and student-centred approaches to support the development of the boys' literacy learning outcomes and specifically knowledge of image and language in stories.

The project was developed from a strengths-based approach by drawing on the boys' prior knowledge from digital text engagement outside of school, as well as their interest areas. The aim was to work towards developing further understanding and knowledge of multimodal text communication (Barton, Arnold & Trimble-Roles, 2015).

DOI: 10.4324/9781003268772-8

As one of the main aims of the project was to support students' understanding of composing multimodal texts given the proliferation of such texts in the ways we communicate (Barton, 2019), we acknowledged that more and more children begin school with extended access to digital technologies (Plowman, 2015). This may mean that they possess a range of outside-of-school literacies that could support their learning (O'Brien & Comber, 2020).

Using technologies has also been noted to increase engagement and motivation, particularly for boys (Watson, Kehler & Martino, 2010), so we wanted to use digital technologies in the project to support the boys' literacy learning (Oakley et al., 2020). As such, the focus research question for this project was: How can kinaesthetic and student-centred approaches to learning support boys' literacy learning (and specifically multimodal text composition) development?

The importance of learning and teaching multimodal text communication

Much research investigates how educators are required to best prepare their students for an unpredictable workforce in the future (Barton, 2023). Indeed, back in 2016, a news report highlighted how children and students of today need to be taught a range of skills from computing programming, communication via a range of modes, and alternative ways of thinking for the production and consumption of resources (ABC, 2016), labeling an approach as *Future Proof*. In some respects, this urgency to educate differently is counter to research that argues children and young people are increasingly adept at using a range of technologies – indeed, even more effectively than their parents and teachers (Prensky, 2001) – and that their out-of-school literacies are distinct from those taught in school (Skerrett & Bomer, 2011).

In our work, we have found many children do have the necessary capabilities to use digital technologies effectively to communicate meaning yet they need to develop the necessary metalanguage associated with this multimodal communication to better express this knowledge.

In our study, we implemented a pedagogical approach that addressed Kress and van Leeuwen's three meta-semiotic resources. These are what we need in order to both comprehend (read) or compose (create) multimodal texts. The first is representational meaning, which involves what the subject matter is in any text. This could include an image or images, the information conveyed during a performance or language resources involved in print-based texts. The second is interpersonal meaning, which is about how different modes interact with a reader or viewer or audience. Interpersonal meaning involves emotions and aesthetics and how multimodal texts make us think and feel. Finally, compositional meaning, which includes the ways in which the author and/or artist has composed their text through the use of cohesion (Kress & van Leeuwen, 2006) and how they manipulate specific media differently and appropriately. We use these three meta-semiotic meanings to guide the learning, specifically in relation to visual image.

When we consider young children's multimodal learning we can see that they create their own understanding of the world around them through active exploration of their environments and interaction with others (The Queensland Studies Authority, 2006). In a similar way, the use of objects and representations can help enhance children's understanding, as this invites awareness, investigation, manipulation, explanation, experimentation, and imagination (Bronfenbrenner & Morris, 1998). Elliott (2006) found that high-quality and equitable early life experiences are important as they assist children to overcome the effects of being disadvantaged and allow them to excel in learning in general. Therefore, it is important for teachers to consider kinaesthetic approaches to learning when developing literacy programmes (Arnold, 2021; Barton, 2015, 2019). Promoting equitable access for all students through physically based learning and those that value prior knowledge is critical for success (Nxumalo & Delgado Vintimilla, 2020). Equitable access can assist the scaffolding process for young literacy learners ensuring that the children's foundation areas of literacy learning are on an equal level.

As highlighted previously, literacy no longer involves just reading and writing. Advances in technology have changed and expanded the ways in which we perceive literacy. Makin, Jones Diaz, and McLachlan (2007) define multiliteracy as multimodal ways of communicating through linguistic, visual, auditory, gestural and spatial forms and explained further that multiliteracy also involves the integration of computer technology and literacy. It is important to consider different types of literacies for young children given they have diverse personal, social and cultural experiences prior to school (Hill, 2019).

Multiliteracies include digital literacies, technoliteracies, electronic literacies, visual literacies and print-based literacies (Hill, 2006, p. 323).

According to Hill (2006) digital literacy and print-based literacy are therefore not in opposite corners; people in developed societies now need both to become truly literate learners. Similarly, Cope and Kalantzis (2000) define multiliteracy as a multiplicity of literacies for different purposes in different contexts. Lankshear, Gee, Knobel, and Searle (1997) assert that the dynamic nature of language and society requires people to embrace new and specific social practices continuously.

In the context of our study, we aimed to adopt a holistic approach when teaching literacy to young learners in modern society. Cumming-Potvin (2007) suggests that although children are capable of constructing their identity as literacy learners, they also benefit from social interaction and tasks. Multiliteracies that interweave scaffolding, diverse texts and meaningful tasks can become powerful agents for students' learning (Barton & Trimble-Roles, 2018).

Using digital technologies and arts-based and kinaesthetic approaches in supporting the boys to learn more about visual literacy and the composition of multimodal texts, we argue, provided them with a solid foundation of critical literacy experiences and social practices.

Context of the study

The school involved in this study was located in a low socio-economic outer suburb of Brisbane, Queensland, Australia. The boys (n = 6) involved in the project were in the Preparatory year of school and had a full-time teacher aide and an Early Childhood specialist teacher. These boys were selected due to needing support in the area of literacy education. Although the school had invested in technology, it was only a 1–1 device school from Year 5 upwards. In the Prep classroom there were eight iPads available for educational use for the entire class. The boys in this group used an iPad in pairs.

Research design

To answer the overarching and sub-questions we employed a Learning by Design (LbD) (Kalantzis & Cope, 2005) approach in the classroom involving four knowledge processes. These are: experiencing the known and new;

conceptualising by naming and theorising; analysing functionally and crit-ically; and applying appropriately and creatively (Kalantzis & Cope, 2005). The first stage of a LbD approach is acknowledging the skills and experi-ence children bring with them into the classroom space. Next, students are supported to develop a deeper knowledge of the topic at hand. They do this by naming, classifying, grouping and linking information. Third, students investigate the value and impact of new knowledge and finally, they present and communicate their learnings in novel and unique ways.

Learning by Design views a classroom as an ecosystem, a community where both teachers and students are learners and teachers. Students are viewed as equal contributors to education meaning they should have some choice in what they learn. To do this, teachers need to plan for a variety of learning activities such as experimentation, classroom discussion, time to explore, trial and error etc. As such, our approach was to support the boys to approach their learning in a way that engaged and motivated them to know more.

Aligning with curriculum expectations

When developing the process for supporting the boys' learning, curric-ulum content descriptions were identified. These were selected from the *Australian Curriculum: English* and related to multimodal text composition. See Box 1:

BOX 1

Language
Understand concepts about print and screen, including how books, film and simple digital texts work, and know some features of print, for example directionality (ACELA1433).

Explore the different contributions of words and images to meaning in stories and informative texts (ACELA1786).

Literature
Foundation: Retell familiar literary texts through performance, use of illustrations and images (ACELT1580).

Identify some features of texts including events and characters and retell events from a text (ACELT1578).

Literacy

Construct texts using software including word processing programmes (ACELY1654).

The process

As highlighted above our study was guided by the Learning by Design (Kalantzis & Cope, 2005) approach as well as Early Years learning philosophies including notions of independence and agency (Australian Government Department of Education and Training, n.d.). The Queensland Studies Authority (2006) affirms that children create individual understandings through their active exploration of their environments and their interactions with people, objects and representations. Bronfenbrenner and Morris (1998) found that the use of objects and representations helps to enhance children's understanding, as this invites awareness, investigation, manipulation, explanation, experimentation, and imagination. Elliott (2006) found that high-quality and equitable early life experiences are important for children, particularly as they may be vital for assisting children to overcome the effects of being disadvantaged.

In order to provide high-quality literacy programmes, we ensured that our study incorporated and promoted equitable access to all of these factors in order to create optimal opportunities for learning literacy. Providing children with a solid foundation of literacy experiences and social practices gave them the opportunity to develop despite having some challenges in literacy. Table 8.1 outlines the phases involved in the learning and teaching process with the boys.

Phase A

In this phase of the study, we were interested in knowing how much the boys already knew about how images convey meaning. As such, we selected a range of award-winning books that were age appropriate for the boys to explore. The books also featured quality narrative structures, knowledge

Table 8.1 Phases of learning and teaching

Phase	Steps
A. Drawing on prior knowledge	1. Exploring prior knowledge about visual grammar/literacy by showing the boys well-known children's literature that they could connect with and discuss
B. Building the field	2. Identifying with the students the process of the project 3. Identifying sequences of well-known texts 4. Drawing a sequence
C. Introducing new concepts	1. Exploring elements of image through picture books 2. Character portrayal through image in a story 3. Exploring interpersonal meaning/identifying the feelings 4. Drawing characters from different perspectives
D. Applying the knowledge	5. Creating photographs with different camera angles, shots, framing and light 6. Identifying and selecting the images to use in a short story 7. Creating the digital story – words/sentences that match the images, add the images, add the text, create and add the voice over
E. Celebrating and evaluating	8. Share the achievements 9. Reflect on the work

they would need in the final phase of the research. The books used in Phase A were:

- *Big Rain Coming* by Katrina Germein
- *Fox* by Margaret Wild
- *My Best Friend Bob* by Georgie Ripper
- *Grandpa and Thomas* by Pamela Allen
- *The Little Refugee* by Anh Do

The boys were read the stories and were then asked to select individual pages to describe in relation to what the pictures were telling us. Prompt questions were used to gauge the boys' understanding of the three meta-semiotic meanings, that is, subject matter, the effect of how they make us feel, and layout.

Generally, the boys had extensive knowledge about how images evoke meaning for the viewer. As a group, the boys worked together to imagine ideas through inference from each of the pages. They also related the images to their own experiences frequently, emphasising the point that when reading children need to make connections between themselves and the texts.

Phase B

To engage the boys with narrative structure we asked them to identify sequences of events in stories. They were learning about nursery rhymes, so the teacher read the story "Jack and Jill" and then the boys were asked to cut and paste the sequence of the story (for permission reasons we are unable to share these images). All students were able to identify the sequence of the story accurately. They also coloured their pictures, which showed they already had some understanding of emotions through the use of colour.

After this activity, the boys then read "Humpty Dumpty" and drew the sequence of the story.

Phase C

The boys were taught about different elements to creating images for effect including colour, camera angles – close-up, mid-shot and long shot, framing, light, focal point, bird's eye view and back or rear-view shots. The boys were read the story "Not now, Bernard!" by David McKee and together we identified the camera angles, shots and colours. We noticed that Bernard's mother and father never looked directly at the reader and always looked tired and cranky. Bernard on the other hand was always looking at the reader (a demand view). They were not sure whether Bernard was the monster or not!

The boys then drew their own monsters with the following in mind:

1. A front view
2. A side view
3. A back view

Phase D

In the final phase of the study, the boys used digital technologies (iPads) to explore their new knowledge about images. They experimented with different types of camera angles, lighting and framed shots with toy dinosaurs. Once they were happy with the photos that they shot they then had to select some to create a storyboard. The storyboard involved the boys understanding the sequencing of a narrative including the orientation, conflict and resolution. Finally, they used the photos they selected to create their own multimodal texts by adding in some language.

Conclusion

Our project began with the question: How can Early Years boys' knowledge of visual literacy and multimodal text composition be improved to better equip them for the future? Through our multi-phase study, we were able to see improvement in the boys' visual literacy understanding and we were also able to draw on their prior knowledge of using technology to create effective multimodal and digital texts. This classroom work significantly addressed a number of areas of the Australian Curriculum: English outcomes while also embracing innovative and progressive thinking in the classroom space for Early Years boys. We strongly believe that targeted learning and teaching sessions on a range of visual features including camera angles, colour, framing and light, can greatly improve Early Years boys' presentation of multimodal texts. Building on their personal strengths and providing them opportunities to express their own identities and agency, we were able to support the learning of technological and 21st-century literacy skills needed now and in the future.

References

Alloway, N., Freebody, P., Gilbert, P., & Muspratt, S. (2002). *Boys and literacy: Expanding the repertoires of practice*. DEST Commonwealth of Australia.

Arnold, J. (2021). *Integrating kinesthetic learning activities to phonics learning*. Unpublished Masters Thesis. University of Wisconsin- River Falls.

Australia Broadcast Corporation (ABC). (2016). *Future Proof. Four Corners*. Retrieved from: www.abc.net.au/4corners/stories/2016/07/04/4491818.htm

Australian Government Department of Education and Training (n.d.) *Belonging, being & becoming: The early years learning framework for Australia*. Australian Government.

Barton, G. M. (2015). Arts-based educational research in the early years. *International Research in Early Childhood Education*, 6(1), 62–78.

Barton, G. M. (2019). *Developing literacy and the arts*. Routledge.

Barton, G. M. (2023). *Aesthetic literacies in school and work: New pathways for education*. SpringerBrief.

Barton, G.M., Arnold, J., & Trimble-Roles, R. (2015). Writing practices today and in the future: Multimodal and creative text composition in the 21st century. In J. Turbill, C. Brock & G. M. Barton (Eds.), *Teaching Writing in Today's Classrooms: Looking Back to Look Forward* (pp. 241–261). ALEA occasional publication July 2015.

Bronfenbrenner, U., & Morris, P.A. (1998). The ecology of developmental processes. In R. M. Lerner (Ed.), *Handbook of Child Psychology, 5th ed.* (pp. 993–1028). Wiley.

Cope, B., & Kalantzis, M. (2000). *Multiliteracies*. New York: Routledge.

Cumming-Potvin, W. (2007). Scaffolding, multiliteracies, and reading circle. *Canadian Journal of Education*, 30(2), 483–507.

Disenhaus, N. (2015). *Boys, writing, and the literacy gender gap: What we know, what we think we know*. The University of Vermont and State Agricultural College.

Elliot, A. (2006). *Early childhood education: Pathways to quality and equity for all children*. Australian Council for Educational Research (ACER).

Fletcher, R. (2000). *Inquiry into the education of boys*. Submission to Parliament of Australia House of Representatives Standing Committee on Employment, Education and Workplace Relations.

Henry, K., Lagos, A., & Berndt, F. (2012). Scholarship-in-practice bridging the literacy gap between boys and girls: An opportunity for the National Year of Reading 2012. *The Australian Library Journal*, 61(2), 143–150.

Hill, S. E. (2006). *Developing early literacy: Assessment and teaching*. Eleanor Curtain.

Hill, S. E. (2019). Early literacy: A multimodal process. *Handbook of research on the education of young children* (pp. 113–122). Routledge.

Kalantzis, M., & Cope, B. (2005). *Learning by design*. Common Ground.

Kress, G., & Van Leeuwen, T. (2006). *Reading images: The grammar of visual design*. Routledge.

Lankshear, C., Gee, J., Knobel, M., & Searle, C. (1997). *Changing literacies*. Buckingham, UK: Open University Press.

Makin, L., Jones Diaz, C., & Lachlan, L. (2007). *Literacies in childhood: Changing views, challenging practice* (2nd ed.). Marrickville, NSW: Elsevier.

Millard, E. (2002). *Differently literate: Boys, girls and the schooling of literacy*. Routledge.

Moss, G., & Washbrook, L. (2016). Understanding the gender gap in literacy and language development. Bristol Working Papers in Education. University of Bristol.

Nxumalo, F., & Delgado Vintimilla, C. (2020). Explorations of the tensions and potentials of de-centering the human in early childhood education research. *Equity & Excellence in Education, 53*(3), 271–275.

Oakley, G., Wildy, H., & Berman, Y. E. (2020). Multimodal digital text creation using tablets and open-ended creative apps to improve the literacy learning of children in early childhood classrooms. *Journal of Early Childhood Literacy, 20*(4), 655–679.

O'Brien, J., & Comber, B. (2020). Negotiating critical literacies with young children. In C. Barratt-Pugh & M. Rohl (Eds.), *Literacy Learning in the Early Years* (pp. 152–171). Routledge.

Plowman, L. (2015). Researching young children's everyday uses of technology in the family home. *Interacting with Computers, 27*(1), 36–46.

Prensky, M. (2001). Digital natives, digital immigrants. *On the Horizon, 9*(5), 1–6.

Queensland Studies Authority (2006). *Early years curriculum guidelines*. Brisbane, Queensland: Queensland Government.

Skerrett, A. & Bomer, R. (2011). Borderzones in adolescents' literacy practices. Urban Education, *46* (6), 1256–1279. doi:10.1177/0042085911398920

Trimble-Roles, R., & Barton, G. (2018). A child-centred approach to multimodal text composition in the early years. *Practical Literacy: The Early and Primary Years, 23*(3), 39–43.

Watson, A., Kehler, M., & Martino, W. (2010). The problem of boys' literacy underachievement: Raising some questions. *Journal of Adolescent & Adult Literacy, 53*(5), 356–361.

Building a bridge

LEGO as a kinaesthetic tool to facilitate play-based learning in Early Childhood and beyond

Melissa Fanshawe, Monique Mandarakas, Melissa Cain, Michelle Turner, Marie White, Marie Oddoux, Marc Angelier and Per Havgaard

Introduction

Early Childhood Education and Care (ECEC) has had a lengthy history of drawing on play as a rich context for children's learning and engagement within the world (Nadolinskaya, 2015). A focus on the holistic development of students considers play as the recommended approach for Early Childhood contexts internationally (United Nations Educational Organisation [UNESCO] 2016). Within Australia, *The Early Years Learning Framework* (EYLF) introduces play as a pedagogy for learning that involves active engagement with people, objects and representations (Department of Education Employment and Workplace Relations [DEEWR], 2009). The EYLF highlights the importance of play as a pedagogical strategy and a vehicle for the expression of agency for children, promoting active engagement in learning (DEEWR, 2009).

DOI: 10.4324/9781003268772-9

Despite the known benefits of play-based learning, play is not purpose-fully implemented in all Australian schools, and many teachers in school settings are unaware of how play-based learning can be used to support children's academic and social development (Barblett et al., 2016). This may stem from a lack of training or professional development around what play-based learning looks like in a school environment (Gray & Ryan (2016). A better understanding of play-based learning may provide educators an awareness of how play can be used within the early years of school to facilitate holistic development for children (Parker et al., 2022).

Underpinning play-based learning is the importance of kinaesthetic experiences (the use of touch and movement) to help children become immersed in learning. Children learn best when they are active (Lundqvist et al., 2019), and engaged with materials that are meaningful to them and promote opportunities or creativity (Weisberg et al., 2013). However, these experiences do not just occur incidentally, as careful design of pedagogical practices are required to facilitate optimal experiences (Yelland, 2011).

This chapter considers the benefits of play-based learning for Early Childhood students as they transition into the formal school context. We will uncover the types of play within an umbrella of play-based learning pedagogies and how we use and assess play within the classroom. We also examine the importance of the student experience of learning outcomes through the design and facilitation of play-based learning experiences. The exploration of the popular children's toy LEGO (Figure 9.1) will be used throughout the chapter as a case study to support the use of kinaesthetic learning tools to bridge the gap for play-based learning between Early Childhood and formal school settings.

Building the foundations

Learning through play?

The importance of learning through play has been highlighted in contemporary research for the holistic development of "cognitive, social, emotional, creative and physical skills through active engagement in learning" (Parker et al., 2022, p. 1). However, the idea of learning through play is so ubiquitous that often the constitution of play and the interaction between the outcomes and the child's experiences are uncertain (Grieshaber & McArdle, 2010). In

Figure 9.1 Image of a bridge made out of LEGO

a meta-analysis of 62 studies undertaken in 24 countries, Bubikova-Moan et al. (2019) found many educators were unsure of what constitutes play and how to best implement it within their own context. The analysis showed multifaceted theoretical influences that underpin play-based learning and identified that teachers, throughout diverse contexts, had different views on what play should look like, and how teacher involvement impacted the effectiveness of play (Bubukova-Moan et al., 2019). This is important, as teachers' underpinning beliefs about play were found to impact their implementation of play-based learning activities (Wu et al., 2018).

In a white paper examining how children learn through play, Zosh et al. (2017) proposed that play-based learning sits under an umbrella of different types of playful learning which are differentiated according to the involvement of the student and the teacher (see Figure 9.2). The umbrella analogy supports educators to understand how play-based learning can consist of a number of different experiences, including free play (child-led), guided play (child-led and adult-scaffolded) and games (adult-led with rules and constraints). Experiences under the umbrella of playful learning were more

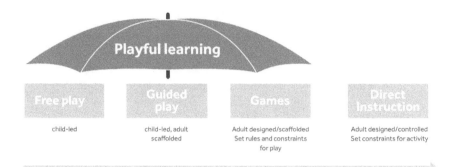

Figure 9.2 Learning through play: a review of the evidence. White paper
Source: Sourced from Zosh et al. (2017).

child-centred than direct instruction, which is not considered play-based learning.

Under the umbrella of playful learning, free play was identified by Zosh et al. (2017) as the most child-led playful learning experience. The importance of free play was highlighted by Ogolla (2018), who undertook a study of 377 pre-school students and found that the availability of suitable play materials and time for free play positively influenced the holistic development of children, specifically with regard to decision-making and social interactions. However, the same study also identified that teachers felt pressure to reduce the time spent on free play, as school leaders prioritised the academic outcomes of students (Ogolla, 2018). This indicates that educators see play as not supportive of academic outcomes, or that they are mutually exclusive.

The findings from the above study align with the work of Marbina et al. (2011) who also identified time limitations for teachers to implement free play due to pressures to meet curriculum outcomes. Further concerns regarding implementing free play in the school setting were found by (Jay & Knaus, 2018), who recognised that teachers feared a lack of control when facilitating learning activities during free play. These pressures and concerns may give insight into why play-based pedagogies have become less utilised in school environments.

"Guided play" and "games" are placed between "free play" and "direct teaching" approaches to encourage children to become active and engaged in the learning experience (Zosh et al., 2017). Within guided play, teachers design the environment and provide suitable materials to stimulate playful experiences that will meet the intended learning outcomes (Weisberg et al., 2013). Guided play has been found to foster active hands-on learning, scaffold iterative and critical thinking, language development, social, emotional and cognitive development, choice, exploration, curiosity, joy and freedom (Allee-Herndon & Roberts, 2021; Zosh et al., 2017). Games offer a similar child interaction, where teachers provide the materials and instructions and students interact with learning through play-based games, usually with an element of competition. Games are particularly common in physical education to increase gross motor development, problem-solving and social interaction (Makhkamovich, 2021). Games have also been used within classrooms to increase academic performance and cognitive memory (Iasha et al., 2020).

Outside the umbrella of play, is direct instruction, where adults design and deliver the activity. Direct instruction approaches centre on learning experiences where teachers act as controllers, rather than guides and facilitators in learning (Zosh et al., 2017). Direct instructional approaches lack the support of children's agency in learning and can fail to engage them successfully in their learning (Lundqvist et al., 2019). Supporting teachers to understand, devise and teach using play-based learning approaches may help move away from a purely direct instructional model to include a more effective blend of child-led and teacher-led opportunities (Dzamesi & van Heerden, 2020).

Is the inclusion of play in school settings in crisis?

Despite research-based evidence that play-based learning can provide children with academic benefits, play-based learning for Early Childhood students in school contexts is not as evident as teacher-directed learning (Barblett et al., 2016). This can be evidenced by looking at several education systems throughout the world. In Asia for example, there is a high societal focus on academic learning, which places pressure on teachers to achieve curriculum outcomes with play-based learning considered the anthesis of academic learning (Bautista, 2021). In the UK and Canada, policy supports play-based philosophies as a vehicle to support children's transition to school (Fisher, 2021), however, a study by Wickstrom et al. (2019) found the Canadian education system had a misalignment between policies that support play and practices which focused on academic outcomes.

Similarly in Western Australia, policy changes mandated play be included in the early years of the primary curriculum, and for the existing curriculum to work alongside the EYLF (Jay & Knaus, 2018), however, there is still a disparity between policy and practice which needs to be addressed (Fisher, 2021). Fisher (2021) discussed a need for top-down support from the leadership of schools to ensure policies of play were enacted in classrooms. Australian teachers have also reported an erosion of play as pressure from school leaders to focus on national testing measures (for example, the National Assessment Program Literacy and Numeracy [NAPLAN]) has pushed down to the early years of schooling (Barblett et al., 2016; Roberts et al., 2019). Fisher (2021) believes this has resulted in more direct teaching pedagogies and a narrowing of the curriculum to ensure children are adequately prepared for the tests. (Roberts et al., 2019) found that a focus on direct instruction to succeed in high-stake tests failed to serve the needs of diverse learners and had a negative impact on the provision on play-based learning in the early years.

The success of Finnish students in international standardised testing, has led many educators to look at their education system as an exemplar of good practice. In Finland, Early Childhood Education is based on play-based learning, with coexisting systems, structures and training of teachers to focus on play-based pedagogical practices (Ferreira, 2021). Allee-Herndon and Roberts (2021) counter that a focus on high standards and accountability does not need to be seen as separate from play-based learning approaches, which offer children hands-on learning along with rich language development opportunities. This opens a space for hope and a way forward in the early years. Careful consideration of the transition for children, from a play-based approach, in Early Childhood to the school context is required, as the alignment between these contexts has been shown to impact children's future academic and social success at school (Mirkhil, 2010).

The importance of kinaesthetic experiences in Early Childhood

A second key element of play-based learning is the premise that "children develop holistic skills by interacting with people, objects and representations" (Department of Education and Training, 2016) in actively engaging, joyful, iterative, meaningful and socially interactive experiences

(Zosh et al., 2017). Hands-on materials help students develop their conceptual understanding through kinaesthetic experiences (Hsieh & McCollum, 2019). In a study of 20 play-based kindergarten classrooms in suburban and rural contexts in the United States, DeLuca et al. (2020) found that 95% of teachers considered manipulative materials when preparing the environment for play.

Learning through kinaesthetic movement and use of manipulative materials was shown by Marley and Carbonneau (2014) to benefit children by providing opportunities to physically interact with kinaesthetic materials within their environments. Further, kinaesthetic materials provide a brain-body connection, which has been found to increase on-task behaviours, encourage children to take risks, and increase collaboration (McGlynn & Kozlowski, 2017). It was also noted by Marley and Carbonneau (2014) that the use of physical materials and objects help students develop an understanding between concrete and abstract topics, which is important for future learning. Through play, manipulatives and movement required for kinaesthetic learning can be afforded to students to assist in learning (Marsh et al., 2019).

With this research in mind, we ask how can we introduce quality, purposefully selected resources into the environment to support children's learning and development; work alongside them, question them, and celebrate play-based learning (Yelland, 2011).

LEGO in education

LEGO as a kinaesthetic tool provides an opportunity to plan and design quality play-based learning experiences to meet curriculum outcomes, which can traverse educational contexts (United Nations Children's Education Fund [UNICEF], 2018). The use of LEGO as a kinaesthetic tool to stimulate playful experiences has been identified across many curriculum areas and general capabilities. For example, Cvijanović and Mojić (2018) used LEGO in 30 Early Childhood settings to stimulate play activities for children. The research found that LEGO was useful for free play through construction but could also be strategically set up by educators to encourage play-based learning.

Table 9.1 compiles an overview of recent literature which has identified the use of LEGO as a playful kinaesthetic tool in Early Childhood. It

Table 9.1 Use of LEGO in educational literature: Play with LEGO

English
- Supported greater communication and creativity (Cohen & Emmons, 2017).
- Benefited children's language and social development across cultural contexts (Hsieh & McCollum, 2019).
- Supported literacy and numeracy outcomes (McDonald & Howell, 2012).

Mathematics
- Linked to the proficiency strands to help children to move beyond procedural understanding to see concrete strategies and combinations (Petersson & Weldemariam, 2022).
- Supported logical and divergent thinking, mental imagery and non-verbal reasoning (Pirrone et al., 2018).
- Developed conceptual understanding, – young children, aged three-four, could count, count on, use language "more than less than", match numerals to numbers, determine rectangular numbers, make arrays, group in sets, produce patterning at much higher levels than expected for their age and supported the beginning of symbolic language for addition and subtraction (McDonald & Howell, 2012; Peterson & Treagust, 2014; Petersson & Weldemariam, 2022; Simoncini et al., 2020)
- Highlighted the links between 2D to 3D (Cowan, 2018).
- Focused on mathematic concepts, e.g., geometry and spatial and positional language, the links between 2D and 3D (Cohen & Emmons, 2017; Cowan, 2018; Hsieh & McCollum, 2019; McDonald & Howell, 2012).
- Supported the use of informal uniform units of measurement (McDonald & Howell, 2012; Preston, 2017).

Science and Technology
- Explored physics, the effects of large and small forces on motion (Preston, 2017).
- Helped children to engage in playful learning and meaning boundaries between digital and non-digital forms (Cowan, 2018).
- Supported hands on 21st Century learning to use creative technologies rather than pre-programmed apps (McDonald & Howell, 2012).

Social, Emotional and Behavioural
- Increased social and behavioural regulation skills (Hsieh & McCollum, 2019; McDonald & Howell, 2012; Zosh et al., 2017).
- Supported increase in emotional engagement – through guided play with LEGO (Petersson & Weldemariam, 2022).

Table 9.1 Cont.

Inclusion and diversity
• Supported interventions with the potential to maximise motivation and social interactions (Hu et al., 2018).
• Supported early math learning in low income countries as it is a cheap, effective resource to train teachers to use (Simoncini et al., 2020).
• Supported children from disadvantaged, NESB and Indigenous backgrounds to remediate the gap they face when entering school (McDonald & Howell, 2012).
• Promoted increased social initiations and responses through use of peer mediated LEGO play in EC for children, with Autism (Hu et al., 2018).
• Recognised the impact play spaces might have on creating binary divisions and take a post humanist perspective to consider different ways of being (Lyttleton-Smith, 2019).
• Used maker spacers are places that can support children who have not had access to technology (Bers et al., 2018).

recognises the role in English, mathematics, science and technology, along with the use in developing social, emotional, and behavioural characteristics. The literature also reveals the use of LEGO to facilitate inclusion within play, through the use of LEGO as a manipulative in low-income populations (Simoncini et al., 2020) and for students with disability (Hu et al., 2018).

Therefore, this brings rise to the question as to how can we use kinaesthetic tools, such as LEGO, to help teachers bridge the gap between meeting school prioritised curriculum outcomes, while allowing the place of play for Early Childhood students (Walsh et al., 2019). To answer this question, we first look at how educators can develop a common understanding of play, to promote the use of play-based pedagogies in school contexts.

Laying the conceptual structure of kinaesthetic learning

To support educators to find a common understanding of the components of a play-based approach in classrooms, Parker and Thomsen (2019) proffered a framework which identifies four components of quality learning through play (refer to Figure 9.3). These components consist of design (including materials), outcomes, facilitation (child-led, teacher-guided, or teacher-led) and the child's experience of learning through play. Parker and Thomsen's

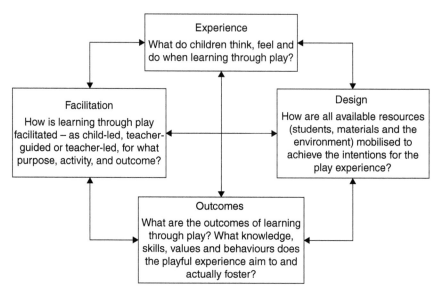

Figure 9.3 Framework for quality learning through play

Source: (Parker & Thomsen, 2019). Sourced from Parker et al. (2022, p. 8).

(2019) framework, considers the umbrella of different types and purposes of play and the agency it provides to children.

Experience

While much of the literature focuses on how educators can design lessons to stimulate playful experiences with kinaesthetic manipulatives, less has been written on the experience of the child within play-based learning. Children reported that they valued play, they did not like it when circle times were "boring" (p. 957), they needed to feel a sense of belonging, they wanted a sense of speed, excitement and physical challenges, to know about the world, to have agency and close connections to family and nature (Lundqvist et al., 2019). Children's points of view about their own experiences are important and assist students to voice their opinions, promoting agency in their learning (Lundqvist et al., 2019).

To assess the intrinsic value of the playful experience for children, The LEGO Foundation (2020) have created *The Learning through Play Experience* tool. This tool contains descriptions of play which educators can use to observe how children are interacting with LEGO manipulatives in play-based activities. *The Learning Through Play Experience* tool recognises six states of play: non-play, passive, exploring, owning, recognising and transferring. It is suggested that educators can observe children within play-based learning activities and code their engagement using the six states of play. The states of play are mapped against the expectations for playful learning, which identify if children appear to find the experiences actively engaging, joyful, iterative, meaningful and socially interactive (Zosh et al., 2017). It is anticipated that focusing on the child's experience will provide educators with information which will guide their design and facilitation of future activities.

The "state of play" coding aligns with the development of the child as they progress through the process of learning. The first state; "non-play" identifies when children are not participating in the activity and the second, a "passive state of play", are following instructions but may be neutral about the experience, or not finding meaning in the activity. This could be that children are not wanting to work in the social group, are distracted from learning, or are not in a social-emotional state to participate in play. However, non-play or passive play could also be because students are not interested in the kinaesthetic materials or the design of the activity.

When identifying non-play or passive play allows us to understand the experience of the student and address this in the design and facilitation. For example, a recent study by the LEGO Group (2021) surveyed nearly 7,000 US parents on their views on society's gender stereotypes for playing with LEGO. The results found that parents were less likely to give girls LEGO than boys and "over 8 times as likely to think of engineers as men than women (89% vs. 11%)" (p. 1). This prompts us to consider the role of gender in play spaces and how we can address this.

When children are exploring, they are curious and interested in kinaesthetic materials and the environment in which they are situated. They are more able to attend to the experience and others around them. Research by (Hsieh & McCollum, 2019; McDonald & Howell, 2012; Zosh et al., 2017) all showed how activities with LEGO were designed to increase spatial awareness in early intervention groups. Through using LEGO, young children became curious about shapes and were deeply engaged with using the kinaesthetic tools to explore shapes in the environment. In turn, the children were able to develop skills that aligned to the mathematics curriculum (Hsieh & McCollum, 2019). This example shows how using manipulatives to design play-based learning can use curiosity to explore learning.

If a child was coded as "owning", they would be enjoying the process, even if it was challenging. A study by Pirrone et al. (2018) examined block play with LEGO with six-year-old children in a primary school context. The activities were seen by the children as a game but were indeed carefully considered learning activities to develop "higher-order thinking skills, academic knowledge, and communication skills" (p. 41). The results of Pirrone et al.'s (2018) study found that the use of kinaesthetic materials helped students focus on developing understanding of challenging concepts in the classroom.

When children are in the "recognising" state of play, they are invested, interact with others, and are deliberate about choices. Cowan (2018) looked at experiences of engaging with three LEGO activities in LEGO House in Billund, Denmark. The article highlighted the collaboration that incidentally occurs through play-based activities which require cooperation and decision-making. Similarly, McDonald and Howell (2012) found that the kinaesthetic learning reinforced social-emotional interactions such as sharing "which is hard for anyone at this age but particularly for children who come from homes where it's not a priority to make them share…so it really reinforces the waiting for turn" (p. 649). These studies demonstrate kinaesthetic materials can encourage social development and learning through child-led interactions in play-based learning.

The final stage occurs after the playful learning activity if the student reflects on the experience and transfers knowledge and skills gained to understand new things. McDonald and Howell (2012) used LEGO robotics in a small primary school in Australia with the aim of teaching basic programming to 5-to-7-year-old children over a 6-week period. The study showed that students developed literacy and numeracy standards through counting parts, direct comparison and positional language, as well as specific terminology and vocabulary about coding throughout the play-based activities. Students were observed throughout the process and were found to be able to transfer knowledge and skills gained to the next activity. This example shows how careful design of activities using kinaesthetic materials can develop students' knowledge and skills which are transferable to other environments.

Design

The second element of the Framework for Quality Learning Through Play (Parker & Thomsen, 2019) is "the design of available resources to achieve the intentions for the play experience" (Figure 9.4). This is where educators consider the management of the environment, the kinaesthetic materials and how children will engage with them to meet the learning outcomes (Parker et al., 2022). Self-directed play with materials increases students' ability to learn through being able to have experimentation with concrete kinaesthetic experiences, which can help students make connections with abstract concepts (Kolb & Kolb, 2018). Conscious design of the materials, environment and the child and teacher's role in the learning experience, may help to bridge play-based pedagogies to the outcomes required in the formal school context (Parker et al., 2022).

Teachers need to have resources and tools to help guide children in play and ensure the children are owning, recognising, and transferring their experiences. LEGO (and Duplo) have been cited as kinaesthetic materials which are low-cost and easily accessible for many groups of learners (Dzamesi & van Heerden, 2020). The LEGO Foundation has also developed LEGO Braille Bricks to increase accessibility of LEGO for students who are blind or have low vision. Sites such as www.sixbrickseducation.com/ help teachers to support the application of LEGO and develop core understandings of the curriculum across the disciplines (Pei-Ying et al., 2021). Considered design of learning experiences using kinaesthetic tools can ensure children learn about outcomes in a meaningful way (Zosh et al., 2017).

Outcomes

Quality experiences designed with play-based pedagogies have been shown to have positive outcomes on the holistic development when children are engaged in the learning (Parker et al., 2022). The positive impacts on learning and development of play-based approaches to learning have also been evidenced in the literature, which included:

- Supporting the development of agency, motivation, engagement and creativity in learning (Fisher, 2021; Walsh et al., 2019)
- Allowing children to see themselves as capable learners (Marsh et al., 2019)
- Improved literacy and numeracy outcomes (Allee-Herndon & Roberts, 2021; McGuinness et al., 2014; Walsh et al., 2019)

- Helping children to develop self-regulatory skills and supported positive behaviour (Weisberg et al., 2013)
- Permitting assessment without intrusion (Walsh et al., 2019)
- Providing a focus on cross-curricula learning to develop real-world connections (Walsh et al., 2019)
- Offered children hands-on, problem-based learning (Allee-Herndon & Roberts, 2021).

The use of kinaesthetic materials within the design of play-based learning has shown to be successful in assisting students to develop conceptual understanding of more abstract concepts. For example, a study by Petersson and Weldemariam (2022) used LEGO cars to design a play-based activity focused on the abstract concept of rectangular numbers. The activity was designed on a real-life concept using LEGO cars and ferries, made from LEGO bricks. The teacher acted as a facilitator and also moderated if any groups had misunderstanding. Using kinaesthetic tools aided students to make decisions about figurative numbers as it provided the opportunity to gain feedback through the materials and the ability to visualise concrete strategies and combinations. The activity included problem-solving, decision-making and group interaction to make meaning of the mathematical concept (Petersson & Weldemarium, 2022). It is apparent that play-based learning can provide rich learning experiences for students.

Within Australia, the Early Years Learning Framework (EYLF) (DEEWR, 2009) recommends play as a pedagogy for learning for all Early Childhood students (within Early Years and school contexts). To support teachers to understand how the five learning outcomes of the EYLF align to the states of play (LEGO Foundation, 2020) we have created a table which maps these elements (Table 9.2). It is important to note that children's learning is ongoing, cyclic, and not linear, and different children will have diverse experiences of the same activities and at different times.

According to Nicholson (2019), a problem exists as there is a misalignment between the EYLF (DEEWR, 2009) and the pedagogy children experience when they transition to school. In the school context, there is additional pressure to align learning experiences to the curriculum, which has been seen as a barrier for implementing play-based philosophies in the classroom (Allee-Herndon & Roberts, 2021; Ogolla, 2018).

Table 9.2 Alignment of the EYLF and the states of play

	Examples of states of play	Evident when children:
Non-Play: Not inspired by the experience or afraid	**Outcome 1: Children have a strong sense of identity** Children learn to interact in relation to others with care, empathy, and respect	*Have not yet shown an interest in the activity or other children*
Passive: I am following instructions	**Outcome 3: Children have a strong sense of wellbeing** Children become strong in their social and emotional wellbeing	*Show an increasing capacity to understand, self-regulate and manage their emotions in ways that reflect the feelings and needs of others*
Exploring: I am considering possibilities	**Outcome 4: Children are confident and involved learners** Children develop dispositions for learning such as curiosity cooperation, confidence, creativity, commitment, enthusiasm, persistence, imagination and reflexivity	*Follow and extend their own interests with enthusiasm, energy and concentration*
Owning: I am choosing my own path	**Outcome 2: Children are connected with and contribute to their world** Children become socially responsible and show respect for the environment	*Participate with others to solve problems and contribute to group outcomes*

(continued)

Table 9.2 Cont.

Recognising: I have new insights	Outcome 5: Children are effective communicators Children interact verbally and non-verbally with others for a range of purposes	Use language to communicate thinking about quantities to describe attributes of objects and collections and to explain mathematical ideas
Transferring: I am reflecting on how this experience can influence the reality of my own life and have confidence that changes myself and others	Outcome 4: Children are confident and involved learners Children transfer and adapt what they have learned from one context to another	Use the process of play reflection and investigation to solve problems

Source: (DEEWR, 2009).

Facilitation

The facilitation of the learning activity by the teacher is crucial to the success of a play-based learning experience. The diverse role of the teacher in implementing play-based pedagogy was also noted by Sundberg et al. (2016), who identified the teacher's role in intervening while children were playing, could lie on a continuum from supervising behaviour, to interacting through questioning the children's activities, navigating collaborate play and sparking curiosity. A recent study by Wu et al. (2018) showed that teachers who had a philosophy of free play, encouraged students to initiate activities and show agency in their learning. Pyle et al. (2018) identified teachers who implemented variations between free play, where students engaged in play-based activities of their own choosing, and structured play, where teachers provided more direct guidance which facilitated play-based learning to meet intended learning outcomes.

Altering between adult-directed play-based activities and child-led activities is also possible within learning experiences. This non-binary approach to play-based learning was evident in the research of Preston (2017), who also designed a LEGO car race to develop scientific inquiry skills around motion. The multi-phase design enabled children to make a car, engage in free play activities to explore the kinaesthetic properties, and then were guided to compare the distance the car travelled. Pirrone et al. (2018) also used a blend of free play and guided play to facilitate play-based learning. A game approach was designed by Petersson and Weldemariam (2022) who set the students a task for which they used LEGO manipulatives to complete the task. The teacher acted as a facilitator of the experience and moderated any misunderstandings. In the activity, the teachers were able to step back as children were able to work in teams and use kinaesthetic materials to check if their answers were correct. The importance of giving children autonomy in their learning was reinforced by Cowan (2018) who noted in her findings, that "deeply important learning can happen in informal times and places that are not positioned as direct acts of teaching" (p. 11). Thus, an important role of the teacher is to design which type of facilitation will enable students to have the greatest experience to meet the outcomes of the play-based activity.

Observation

Although not in the original *Framework for Quality Learning Through Play* by Parker and Thomsen (2019), we wish to highlight the importance of observation and the role it can play to bring the four elements together. Figure 9.4

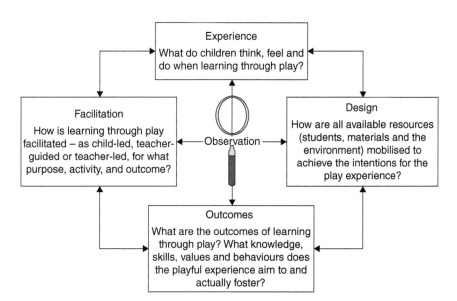

Figure 9.4 Revised framework for quality learning through play
Source: Based on Parker & Thomsen (2019).

shows the inclusion of observation to reflect on the design, outcomes, and facilitation on the students' experience.

Play and a kinaesthetic approach to learning: Bridging the gap between educational contexts

The current body of research raises the question; is play in crisis? Children are seen to leave the contexts of pre-school education, guided by the EYLF (DEEWR, 2009) and through which play is a rich vehicle used to support learning, to enter the school context with an outcomes-based approach where play has been seen to be eroded (Barblett et al., 2016). Postlewaight's (2018) research explored the role reflection might play here to support teachers to consider how the prior-to-school and school curriculum aligned to ensure they were used alongside each other. They argued that children do not change the moment they enter school so neither should our pedagogical approach to ensure successful transition (Postlewaight, 2018). However, consideration is warranted as to how teachers are prepared to support play-based approaches in the early years of school and the barriers they may face when endeavouring to seek alignment between curricula as children transition.

We argue that play-based pedagogies can be aligned with curriculum outcomes with considered design. For example, in Australia, Goal 1 of *The Alice Springs (Mparntwe) Education Declaration* (Council of Australian Governments Education Council, 2019) it is suggested educators provide "varied, challenging, and stimulating learning experiences and opportunities that enable all learners to explore and build on their individual abilities, interests, and experiences" (p. 5). Using kinaesthetic materials, such as LEGO, educators can design learning activities that align to the Australian Curriculum in curriculum areas such as English, maths, science, HASS, the arts and technologies, along with the general capabilities such as literacy, numeracy, critical and creative thinking and personal and social capability (Australian Curriculum Assessment and Reporting Authority [ACARA], 2014) as shown in Table 9.2. These aligned outcomes may have the potential to provide the quantifiable support administrators need to support play-based learning in the early years of school (McGuinness et al., 2014).

Conclusions and implications for practice

A recent push to preference "academic outcomes" as measured through national standardised testing in many countries as well as incorporation of digital learning (Ferreira, 2021) has led to play being considered in some contexts as counterproductive to "serious" learning and having a limited role in meritocratic societies. This chapter has demonstrated, however, that play is crucial for developing peer-to-peer engagement and interpersonal relationships, providing opportunities for embodied imagination and creative thought, as well as the development of self-regulation, motivation to learn, language skills, literacy and numeracy skills, and a sense of agency in learning.

At present, play may be considered a "loosely defined buzzwork" (Bautista et al., 2021, p. 314) in contemporary Early Childhood Education, as the notion of play is rarely defined in education policies. This chapter has successfully mapped the characteristics of play-based learning from teacher-directed play to free play. This chapter has also aligned the components of quality play-based learning with the expectations of the EYLF (DEEWR, 2009) by incorporating the use of the LEGO kinaesthetic learning tool to bridge the gap for play-based learning between Early Childhood and formal school settings. In this way, the constituents and benefits of kinaesthetic play are made clear for Early Childhood Education stakeholders. A particular strength of this chapter is learning about play from the student's perspective by focusing on the element of the "experience" which is often neglected.

This model has strong merits for implementation globally but may be limited by a number of factors. Firstly, the mindset around the value of play in Early Childhood learning which may hinge on cultural perceptions and current societal preferences (particularly in cultures without a social pedagogic tradition); secondly, access to quality Early Childhood Education that uses play-based learning as a pedagogical framework, and thirdly, access to and time with kinaesthetic manipulatives such as LEGO. Whilst initial coding using the tool has been conducted (LEGO Foundation; UNICEF, 2018), further research is needed to support the use of this tool in classroom settings and the authors call for studies to provide an evidence base in educational contexts.

References

Allee-Herndon, K. A., & Roberts, S. K. (2021). The power of purposeful play in primary grades: Adjusting pedagogy for children's needs and academic gains. *Journal of Education (Boston, Mass.), 201*(1), 54–63. https://doi.org/10.1177/0022057420903272

Australian Curriculum Assessment and Reporting Authority [ACARA]. (2014). *General capabilities – General capabilities in the Australian Curriculum – The Australian Curriculum V8.4. [online].* bit.ly/3INfaFk

Barblett, L., Knaus, M., & Barratt-Pugh, C. (2016). The pushes and pulls of pedagogy in the early years: Competing knowledges and the erosion of play-based learning, *Australasian Journal of Early Childhood, 41*(4), 36–43. https://doi.org/10.3316/informit.619041648336775

Bautista, A., & Ho, Y. L. (2021). Music and movement teacher professional development: An interview study with Hong Kong kindergarten teachers. *Australasian Journal of Early Childhood, 46*(3), 276–290.

Bers, M. U., Strawhacker, A., & Vizner, M. (2018). The design of early childhood makerspaces to support positive technological development: Two case studies. *Library Hi Tech, 36*(1), 75–96. https://doi.org/10.1108/LHT-06-2017-0112

Bubikova-Moan, J., Næss Hjetland, H., & Wollscheid, S. (2019). ECE Teachers' views on play-based learning: a systematic review. *European Early Childhood Education Research Journal, 27*(6), 776–800.

Cohen, L. E., & Emmons, J. (2017). Block play: spatial language with preschool and school-aged children. *Early Child Development and Care, 187*(5–6), 967–977. https://doi.org/10.1080/03004430.2016.1223064

Council of Australian Governments Education Council. (2019). *Alice Springs (Mparntwe) education declaration.* https://docs.education. gov.au/system/files/doc/other/final_-_alice_ springs_declaration_-_17_february_2020_ security_removed.pdf

Cowan, K. (2018). Multimodal technologies in LEGO house: A social semiotic perspective. *Multimodal Technologies and Interaction, 2*(4), 70. https://doi.org/10.3390/mti2040070

Cvijanović, N., & Mojić, D. (2018). LEGO material in the programme of early childhood and preschool education. *Croatian Journal of Education: Hrvatski časopis za odgoj i obrazovanje, 20*, 25–45.

DeLuca, C., Pyle, A., Valiquette, A., & LaPointe-McEwan, D. (2020). New directions for kindergarten education: Embedding assessment in play-based learning. *The Elementary School Journal, 120*(3), 455–479. https://doi.org/10.1086/707008

Department of Education and Training. (2016). *Victorian Early Years Learning and Development Framework (VEYLDF): For all children from birth to eight years.* Available online at: (accessed July, 2021).

Department of Education Employment and Workplace Relations [DEEWR]. (2009). *Belonging, being & becoming [electronic resource]: the early years learning framework for Australia*. Dept. of Education, Employment and Workplace Relations for the Council of Australian Governments. http://nla.gov.au/nla.arc-109966

Dzamesi, F. E., & van Heerden, J. (2020). A professional development programme for implementing indigenous play-based pedagogy in kindergarten schools in Ghana. *South African Journal of Education, 40*(3), 1–11. https://doi.org/10.15700/saje.v40n3a1793

Ferreira, J. M. (2021). Play-based learning and phenomenon-based learning in the Finnish Early Childhood Education. *Olhares & Trilhas, 23*(3), 1278–1306.

Fisher, J. (2021). To play or not to play: teachers' and headteachers' perspectives on play-based approaches in transition from the Early Years Foundation Stage to Key Stage 1 in England. *Education, 3–13*. https://doi.org/10.1080/03004279.2021.1912136

Gray, C., & Ryan, A. (2016). Aistear vis-à-vis the Primary Curriculum: the experiences of early years teachers in Ireland. *International Journal of Early Years Education, 24*(2), 188–205.

Grieshaber, S., & McArdle, F. (2010). *The Trouble With Play* (1st ed.). McGraw-Hill Education (UK). https://ebookcentral.proquest.com/lib/acu/detail.action?pq-origsite=primo&docID=650307

Hsieh, W.-Y., & McCollum, J. A. (2019). Teachers' perceptions of early math concepts learned from unit blocks: A cross-cultural comparison. *Early Child Development and Care, 189*(12), 1954–1969. https://doi.org/10.1080/03004430.2018.1423562

Hu, X., Zheng, Q., & Lee, G. T. (2018). Using peer-mediated LEGO® play intervention to improve social interactions for chinese children with autism in an inclusive setting. *Journal of Autism and Developmental Disorders, 48*(7), 2444–2457. https://doi.org/10.1007/s10803-018-3502-4

Iasha, V., Al Ghozali, M. I., Supena, A., Wahyudiana, E., Setiawan, B., & Auliaty, Y. (2020). The traditional games effect on improving students working memory capacity in primary schools. Proceedings of the 4th International Conference on Learning Innovation and Quality Education.

Jay, J., & Knaus, M. (2018). *Embedding play-based learning into junior primary (year 1 and 2) curriculum in WA* (Vol. 43). Edith Cowan University. https://doi.org/10.3316/aeipt.219334

Kolb, A., & Kolb, D. (2018). Eight important things to know about the experiential learning cycle. *Australian educational leader, 40*(3), 8–14.

LEGO Group. (2021). *Girls are ready to overcome gender norms but society continues to enforce biases that hamper their creative potential*. www.lego.com/en-us/aboutus/news/2021/september/lego-ready-for-girls-campaign/

Lundqvist, J., Westling Allodi, M., & Siljehag, E. (2019). Values and needs of children with and without special educational needs in early school years: A study of young children's views on what matters to them. *Scandinavian Journal of Educational Research, 63*(6), 951–967. https://doi.org/10.1080/00313831.2018.1466360

Lyttleton-Smith, J. (2019). Objects of conflict: (re) configuring early childhood experiences of gender in the preschool classroom. *Gender and Education, 31*(6), 655–672. https://doi.org/10.1080/09540253.2017.1332343

Makhkamovich, A. Y. (2021). Physical education of senior schools by means of folk moving games. *European Scholar Journal, 2*(11), 70–72.

Marbina, L., Church, A., & Tayler, C. (2011). Practice Principle 6: Integrated teaching and learning approaches. *Victorian Early Years Learning and Development Framework Evidence Paper.*

Marley, S. C., & Carbonneau, K. J. (2014). Theoretical perspectives and empirical evidence relevant to classroom instruction with manipulatives. *Educational Psychology Review, 26*(1), 1–7.

Marsh, J., Wood, E., Chesworth, L., Nisha, B., Nutbrown, B., & Olney, B. (2019). Makerspaces in early childhood education: Principles of pedagogy and practice. *Mind, Culture and Activity, 26*(3), 221–233. https://doi.org/10.1080/10749 039.2019.1655651

McDonald, S., & Howell, J. (2012). Watching, creating and achieving: Creative technologies as a conduit for learning in the early years: Creative technologies in the early years. *British Journal of Educational Technology, 43*(4), 641–651. https://doi.org/10.1111/j.1467-8535.2011.01231.x

McGlynn, K., & Kozlowski, J. (2017). Kinesthetic learning in science. *Science Scope, 40*(9), 24–27. www.proquest.com/scholarly-journals/kinesthetic-learning-scie nce/docview/1911493781/se-2?accountid=14647

McGuinness, C., Sproule, L., Bojke, C., Trew, K., & Walsh, G. (2014). Impact of a play-based curriculum in the first two years of primary school: literacy and numeracy outcomes over seven years. *British Educational Research Journal, 40*(5), 772–795. https://doi.org/10.1002/berj.3117

Mirkhil, M. (2010). "I want to play when I go to school": Children's views on the transition to school from kindergarten. *Australasian Journal of Early Childhood, 35*(3), 134–139. https://doi.org/10.3316/ielapa.008156536834978

Nadolinskaya, T. V. (2015). The play in the context of the history of philosophy, culture and pedagogy. *Obrazovanie i nauka, 7*, 139–153. https://doi.org/10.17853/ 1994-5639-2013-7-139-153

Nicholson, P. (2019). Play-based pedagogy under threat? A small-scale study of teachers' and pupils' perceptions of pedagogical discontinuity in the transition to primary school. *Education, 3–13, 47*(4), 450–461. https://doi.org/10.1080/03004 279.2018.1496124

Ogolla, P. O. (2018). Influence of free play on pre-school children's holistic development in Homa Bay Sub County, Kenya. *International Journal of Educational Policy Research and Review, 5*(3), 48–56.

Parker, R., & Thomsen, B. S. (2019). Learning through play at school: A study of playful integrated pedagogies that foster children's holistic skills development in the primary school classroom. LEGO Foundation. https://research.acer.edu.au/learning_processes/22

Parker, R., Thomsen, B. S., & Berry, A. (2022). Learning through play at school – A framework for policy and practice. *Frontiers in Education (Lausanne)*, 7. https://doi.org/10.3389/feduc.2022.751801

Pei-Ying, W., Sharon, A., & Jacqueline, H. (2021). Let's build a fast car. *Science and Children*, 59(1), 42–46.

Peterson, J., & Treagust, D. (2014). School and university partnerships: The role of teacher education institutions and primary schools in the development of preservice teacher's science teaching efficacy. *Australian Journal of Teacher Education*, 39(9), 153–167.

Petersson, J., & Weldemariam, K. (2022). Prime time in preschool through teacher-guided play with rectangular numbers. *Scandinavian Journal of Educational Research*, 66(4), 714–728. https://doi.org/10.1080/00313831.2021.1910561

Pirrone, C., Tienken, C. H., Pagano, T., & Di Nuovo, S. (2018). The Influence of Building Block Play on Mathematics Achievement and Logical and Divergent Thinking in Italian Primary School Mathematics Classes. *The Educational Forum (West Lafayette, Ind.)*, 82(1), 40–58. https://doi.org/10.1080/00131725.2018.1379581

Postlewaight, G. (2018). Effective transition to school: Integrating philosophy, pedagogy and curriculum. *NZ International Research in Early Childhood Education Journal*, 21(1), 62–75. https://doi.org/10.3316/informit.263220743000054

Preston, C. (2017). Lego car race. *Teaching Science (Deakin West, A.C.T.)*, 63(4), 4–9. https://doi.org/10.3316/informit.296331532925875

Pyle, A., Prioletta, J., & Poliszczuk, D. (2018). The play-literacy interface in full-day kindergarten classrooms. *Early Childhood Education Journal*, 46(1), 117–127.

Roberts, P., Barblett, L., & Robinson, K. (2019). Early years teachers' perspectives on the effects of NAPLAN on stakeholder wellbeing and the impact on early years pedagogy and curriculum. *Australasian Journal of Early Childhood*, 44(3), 309–320. https://doi.org/10.1177/1836939119855562

Simoncini, K., Forndran, A., Manson, E., Sawi, J., Philip, M., & Kokinai, C. (2020). The impact of block play on children's early mathematics skills in rural Papua New Guinea. *International Journal of Early Childhood*, 52(1), 77–93. https://doi.org/10.1007/s13158-020-00261-9

Sundberg, B., Areljung, S., Due, K., Ekström, K., Ottander, C., & Tellgren, B. (2016). Understanding preschool emergent science in a cultural historical context through Activity Theory. *European Early Childhood Education Research Journal*, 24(4), 567–580.

United Nations Children's Education Fund [UNICEF]. (2018). *Learning through play: Strengthening learning through play in early childhood education programmes*. The LEGO Foundation.

United Nations Educational Organization (2016). Global Education Monitoring Report Summary 2016: Education for People and Planet: Creating Sustainable Futures for All. In: United Nations Educational, Scientific and Cultural Organization Paris, France.

Walsh, G., McGuinness, C., & Sproule, L. (2019). "It's teaching ... but not as we know it": using participatory learning theories to resolve the dilemma of teaching in play-based practice. *Early Child Development and Care*, *189*(7), 1162–1173. https://doi.org/10.1080/03004430.2017.1369977

Weisberg, D. S., Hirsh-Pasek, K., & Golinkoff, R. M. (2013). Guided play: Where curricular goals meet a playful pedagogy. *Mind, Brain and Education*, *7*(2), 104–112. https://doi.org/10.1111/mbe.12015

Wickstrom, H., Pyle, A., & DeLuca, C. (2019). Does theory translate into practice? An observational study of current mathematics pedagogies in play-based kindergarten. *Early Childhood Education Journal*, *47*(3), 287–295. https://doi.org/10.1007/s10643-018-00925-1

Wu, S.-C., Faas, S., & Geiger, S. (2018). Chinese and German teachers' and parents' conceptions of learning at play–similarities, differences, and (in) consistencies. *European Early Childhood Education Research Journal*, *26*(2), 229–245.

Yelland, N. (2011). Reconceptualising play and learning in the lives of young children. *Australasian Journal of Early Childhood*, *36*(2), 4–12. https://doi.org/10.1177/183693911103600202

Zosh, J. N., Hopkins, E. J., Jensen, H., Liu, C., Neale, D., Hirsh-Pasek, K., . . . Whitebread, D. (2017). *Learning through play: A review of the evidence*. LEGO Fonden Billund, Denmark.

Embodied scaffolding and kinaesthetic learning in Finnish Early Childhood Education

Jonna Kangas,
Tuulikki Ukkonen-Mikkola and
Heidi Harju-Luukkainen

Introduction

When a person in western society imagines a classroom, most of us tend to visualise a room full of tables and chairs where silent and sometimes bored children sit and listen passively when the teacher presents knowledge by verbalising it. Active and kinaesthetic experiences are hardly part of those memories. This image of learning is in conflict with several well-known theories of learning. For example, Dewey (1938) stated that learning should be doing. According to Dewey (1938), children's learning is, in fact, interaction with their environment using all senses, and they have a solid need to act, explore, wonder, construct, and invent things. A child's growth and development happen all the time and everywhere. Relying on these holistic ideas about learning, Dewey wanted to integrate learning subjects in a way which supported children's learning best. When conducting action research in Finnish Early Childhood Education Centres from 2012–2015 we noticed in our research, that also in the ECEC context children are expected to listen and be able to follow verbal instructions. After this research project, the Finnish ECEC has undergone a big reform, where the legislation and the curricula shaping the everyday practices, interaction and operation culture have been renewed (see Harju-Luukkainen et al., 2022).

DOI: 10.4324/9781003268772-10

In Finland, like in most countries across the world, there are multiple national and international policy documents guiding ECE provision. On the international level, the guiding documents come from the European Commission (1996), the United Nations (1989), and the United Nations Educational, Scientific, and Cultural Organisation (UNESCO) (1994). Further, the content of ECE is guided by the national curriculum for ECE (ages 1–5; FNAE, 2022) and the national curriculum for preschool education (age 6; FNAE, 2014). Additionally, the law of Early Childhood Education (Finnish law of Early Childhood Education 540/2018) declares the child-teacher ratios and the maximum number of children per class (12 toddlers or 21 three- to five-year-olds). Other acts and policy documents guide the work in ECE settings but with a smaller impact on everyday pedagogical work. (Alila et al., 2022). It is also important to note that the Finnish ECE working teams are multi-professional, consisting of professionals with varying combinations of qualifications. The teams consist of at least one teacher with an academic bachelor's degree and two assistant teachers with lower educational degrees.

From these premises, *the aim of this chapter is to create an overview of the kinaesthetic means of action and communication between teachers and children in Early Childhood Education and Care (ECEC) settings in Finland, through the concepts of learning as embodiment and action.* We start this chapter by presenting the Finnish ECEC concept of playful learning which can be seen as an approach that is defined in many ways in the Finnish ECEC context. To reach our aim, we use two research approaches. Firstly, we introduce how kinaesthetic, active and embodied learning are defined in the current three curricula that cover early education in Finland. With the help of systematic content analysis, we describe the core concepts and understanding of kinaesthetic, active and embodied learning. In order to give an overview of the pedagogical practices, with the help of a case study, we demonstrate how teachers in ECEC conceptualise and use kinaesthetic learning through embodiment guidance and scaffolding in their classrooms. At the end of the chapter, we summarise our findings in a visual image and also discuss the implications of the findings.

The playful approach in Finnish ECEC

The concept of kinaesthetic learning can in Finland be understood through the playful learning approach. And further, the playful learning approach can be understood as a holistic and dynamic form of learning (Kangas et al., 2019). The traditional understanding of learning-oriented play was a division between play types such as physical, social, and cognitive games (Moyles et al., 1989). Playful learning includes multimodal concepts or experiences shown by multiple researchers (Kangas & Harju-Luukkainen, 2022; Kangas et al., 2019; Sefton-Green et al., 2015). The playful learning approach is framed through the understanding of both play and learning, and play is viewed in educational practices through modalities of learning and learning through the modalities of play (Kangas & Harju-Luukkainen, 2022). Further, playfulness in education can be understood as "an attitude, an approach and a way of looking at and interacting with the world" (Sefton-Green et al., 2015, p. 6). In this chapter, we will define the concept of kinaesthetic learning through the playfulness approach.

Playfulness is considered to include different aspects of communication, participation, learning, and being in a joined group of learners. The elements of playfulness include features of narration, insight, communication, creativity, embodiment and action (Hyvönen & Ruokamo, 2005). Of these elements of communication, narration and insight are more linked with children's cognitive abilities, while creativity, embodiment and action include motor, social and emotional competencies together with kinaesthetic awareness and abilities (Kangas & Harju-Luukkainen, 2022). In short, narration refers to the use of imagination and story-telling and -making competencies, which are supported by both creativity and communication skills and abilities to listen, negotiate and narrate the experiences forward. Insight is a form of problem-solving competencies and the ability to think creatively "out-of-the-box" (Hyvönen & Ruokamo, 2005).

The conceptualised approach of playfulness in Early Childhood Education combines the learning paradigm with play. Playful learning in the context of ECEC is an approach where the curricula, methods, pedagogical practices and interaction all focus on enabling play and thus provide children with opportunities to learn. From a multidiscipline approach, play has multimodal natures of form in different societies (Whitebread et al., 2012) and further it is a dynamic and dialogical process (Møller, 2015). Play has modalities such as activity, elements of fun, playful communication, and finally adaptations to active learning through tactile and kinaesthetic activities where children are doers, makers and reproducers of learning (Kangas et al., 2019; Harju-Luukkainen et al., 2019). This multimodal and multisensorial approach comes close to Dewey's (1938) idea of learning by doing where children are interacting with their environment through hands-on activities (Kangas & Harju-Luukkainen, 2022). From philosophical origins, playful learning is defined through the shared objectivities of both play and learning. For example, Henricks (1999, p. 258) summarises that on the one hand play and on the other hand learning both:

- are an experience
- have intrinsic rather than extrinsic motives
- involve some level of active engagement
- the process is more important than the outcome.

While the meaning and functions – the reason why is it important – of learning hardly need to be explained in Western society, the play needs to be constantly justified. It has been shown in research that play facilitates creativity, problem-solving skills, and self-initiated and motivation-oriented learning (Sefton-Green et al., 2015). Playful activities and self-initiated play in the learning environment are shown to support the development of self-regulation skills such as goal setting for learning through independent initiatives, enactment into learning activities through creativity and democracy through choice making (Kangas et al., 2015). Active play involves also physical exercises (Hyvönen & Ruokamo, 2005). Finally, play has also been connected with the active agency of children when they had the freedom to be involved in self-initiated activities (Kangas et al., 2019). In this chapter, we use the definition of playful learning by Kangas and Harju-Luukkainen (2022) where it is described through the modalities of development. In Early Childhood Education play is linked with nurturing growth and wellbeing, development, didactical learning oriented through disciplines such as mathematics and language, interaction, and finally active agency. For example, in the growth and wellbeing category, playful learning is understood to create closeness and to open new opportunities for children (Hännikäinen, 2018; Rutanen, 2012), while in the category of discipline-oriented learning, playful teaching can be used to scaffold children's academic competencies and help them to reach pre-set goals (Vartiainen & Kumpulainen, 2020). To sum up, playful learning is constructed through a multidisciplinary understanding of research about learning as a social, psychological and active learning paradigm, where framing playful learning is possible through modalities of learning and learning through the modalities of play (Kangas & Harju-Luukkainen, 2022).

Conceptualising kinaesthetic learning through active and embodied experiences

Another starting point for learning through play lies in embodiment, where the whole body is used in play and the learning processes. Embodiment refers to combining various physical actions with higher cognitive activities like thinking, reasoning, perceiving and reflecting (Price & Rogers, 2004). Physicality, on the whole, is seen as being important for children's wellbeing and academic achievement; for that reason, it is recommended that physical approaches to learning be applied across the curriculum (DuBose et al., 2008). According to Price and Rogers (2004), active learning is created in an environment where children are aware of and understand the physical surroundings where learning experiences are authentic and interactive. Teachers need to design learning activities that would facilitate physical interaction with others and the environment. Different manifestations of embodiment can include, for example, elements of caring, being afraid, excitement, enjoyment, satisfaction, and security, among others. Hyvönen and Ruokamo (2005) have shown how children express their embodiment in many ways, for example, by adopting views on moral issues, by showing caring or lack thereof, by determining objects of desire and by telling stories of both fearfulness and empowerment. The mind of a human being is also understood to be embodied because abstract thoughts and ideas are not isolated from the sensory-motor system (Johnson, 1999). Spoken language is an essential form of communication in almost all societies, but when speaking, guiding, scaffolding, and explaining to others human beings use a lot of non-verbal means of communication such as gestures, facial expressions, and little movements to give weight to their message. In Early Childhood Education teachers' awareness of the non-verbal messages and their competencies to use them through conscious and planned ways is understood to be essential for high-quality teaching (Neill, 2017). The holistic concept of embodiment includes not only the personal experiences, knowhows, and bodily feelings but also the actions and interactions with our body and other people and the environment, including, for example, the spatial awareness and sense of wellbeing (Hyvönen & Ruokamo, 2005).

In non-verbal communication with children, physical interactions have a central role. According to Johansson et al. (2021), teachers in preschool think that their non-verbal interaction and touch benefits children's sense of security and emotional development. Therefore, teachers in Nordic countries use it when building relations with the children and scaffolding and guiding their learning. Teachers were sensitive towards combining the physical care of children with respect for children's independence and physical integrity (Johannson et al., 2021). Sitting on the teacher's lap is one basic form of physical interaction between child and teacher in the Finnish ECEC context (Hännikäinen, 2018). The elements of an embodiment include also action and movement of the body, especially with the younger children participating in everyday ECEC. Gestures and little actions and movements are common ways to share ideas and communicate thoughts. An action is a physical activity that, in view of the other features of playfulness, is connected to experimental learning (Hyvönen & Ruokamo, 2005). For example, even four-year-old children may be willing to "show" with movement and gestures, and not "talk" verbally about their thinking processes when they are excited and motivated (Leinonen & Sintonen, 2014). However, defining this type of learning is demanding, since there are multiple ways to look at the embodiment in action and its connection to children's learning.

Embodiment is related to one of the characteristics of play that is connected with both bodily and verbal interaction (Bodrova, 2008). In Finnish ECEC, play and playfulness include different forms of play. Games that are typically used in ECEC to practise rules with children, provide experiences of embodiment. For example, in a tag children "freeze" when caught and are "released" by touch (Hyvönen & Ruokamo, 2005). Play trains the ability to practise empathy through the experiences of perceiving, interpreting, and reflecting the emotions of others (Bendelow & Mayall, 2002). Imaginary and pretend play enables children to take on different roles and practise different competencies using their body (Hyvönen & Ruokamo, 2005).

Data and methods

The aim of this chapter is to create an overview of the kinaesthetic means of action and communication between teachers and children in ECEC settings in Finland, through the concepts of learning as embodiment and action. In order to reach this aim, we use two methods. We use 1) systematic content analysis and 2) Observation data from a case study from Finland. In research aiming to shed light on something that is not only text-based; utilising merely a singular method is often insufficient for grasping a holistic view of the examined phenomena. Embodiment learning with kinaesthetic and action-based experiences is a holistic and dynamic way of conceptualising educational practices. Multimethodological design where various types of data are set in a dialogue to complement and confirm the findings from each can be implemented in order to provide wider and more in-depth information (Brooker, 2010; Denzin & Lincoln, 2000).

Systematic content analysis of textual data

With the help of systematic content analysis, we analyse textual curriculum data regarding concepts of kinaesthetic, active and embodied learning in Finland. This we do for the recent three curriculums that are covering early education in Finland. With the help of systematic content analysis, we describe the core concepts and understanding of kinaesthetic, active and embodied learning and give readers of this chapter an overview of the curriculum frame of this theme. Research on document sources has applicability in educational sciences, as educational systems consistently produce excessive amounts of documentary data (Punch & Oancea, 2014). For the conceptualisation of embodied, active and kinaesthetic learning in curricula we use literature review. According to Salminen (2011), descriptive literature review is one of the most used basic types of literature review. The materials used are extensive and the selection of materials is not limited by strict methodological rules. However, it is possible to describe the phenomenon under investigation in a broad way and to classify the characteristics of the phenomenon under investigation through descriptions and interpretations of those. The research questions are broader than in a systematic review or meta-analysis. Further, Salminen (2011) argues that methodologically, it is the lightest form of literature review, but with its help, it is possible to give a broad picture of the subject under discussion or to describe the history and development of the subject under discussion. The aim of our data analysis is to analyse and examine the literature to identify and crystallise the main ideas, conceptions and relationships of embodied, active and kinaesthetic learning and teaching (Snyder, 2019).

Case study (observation data)

For reviewing the actual pedagogical practice, we have chosen to use a case-study approach where the data consisted of five teachers' reported practices

143

in an ECE class with children aged 3–5 years. Teachers were asked to report their implementation process considering playful activities and lesson plans. For this chapter, a case especially focusing on the kinaesthetic learning and embodiment. In the first phase of analysis, teachers' descriptions were read and open-coded to identify kinaesthetic and bodily activities offered to children by the teacher. In the second phase, the coded episodes were labelled. The first labelling aimed to point out the kinaesthetic opportunities; the second labelling was focused on the embodiment; and finally, the third labelling was focused on identifying active and playful learning and teaching. In the final phase representative excerpts were chosen from the data to understand how teachers in ECE conceptualise and use kinaesthetic learning through embodiment guidance and scaffolding in their classrooms.

Findings

Finnish curricula

Firstly, we introduce how kinaesthetic, active, and embodied learning are defined in the current three curriculums that cover early education in Finland. Finnish ECEC is guided in accordance with three curriculums: National Core Curriculum for ECEC (FNAE, 2022), National Core Curriculum for Two-Year Pre-Primary Education (FNAE, 2021) and National Core Curriculum for Pre-Primary Education (FNAE, 2014). These normative steering documents are based on the Act on Early Childhood Education and Care (540/2018). These Finnish curriculums emphasise children's active and holistic learning, which combines knowledge, skills, actions, emotions, sensory perceptions, bodily experiences, language and thinking.

With the help of systematic content analysis, we describe the core concepts and understanding of kinaesthetic, active and embodied learning in the curriculums. Through analysis, we identified four categories from the curriculums, which are *bodily learning, bodily interaction, playful learning and physical activity*. These categories can be recognised from all documents.

In curriculums, *bodily learning* is mentioned in two meanings: as children's knowledge of their bodies and learning through bodily activities. Children are guided to respect and protect their own and other bodies. Learning through bodily activities starts from the children's learning environments, they must have possibilities to explore the world with their senses and entire bodies. In learning areas, bodily learning is highlighted especially in diverse forms of expression linked to bodily expression through, for example, drama, dance and play. Additionally, learning by using multiple senses is central to diverse forms of expression.

Bodily interaction is emphasised especially in the learning area called "the rich world of languages". For the learning of interactive skills, the teachers' sensitivity and responsibility to children's non-verbal messages are essential. In addition, sign language can be a way of communication and a teaching language in ECEC.

Playful learning is one main principle and the working method in the Finnish ECEC curriculums. Play promotes the child's learning, development, and wellbeing. Children can learn mathematical thinking, language, interaction and creativity through play. They are for example encouraged to express their mathematical observations and learning by using their body. Furthermore, children have versatile possibilities for natural movement when playing.

Physical activity is mentioned several times in curriculums, and it is defined as a functional working method with children. Physical activity is emphasised especially in the learning area "I grow, move and develop". Children are encouraged to be physically active both indoors and outdoors through guided and independent physical activities, as the natural part of children's day. The goal of physical activity is to develop body management and fundamental movement skills, like balance, locomotor, and manipulative skills. Physical education is regular, goal-oriented, child-focused and versatile.

These categories are all based on the learning concept whereby children are seen as active agents in their learning. Kinaesthetic, active and embodied learning is seen in curriculums as a central part of children's daily activities, and they can be integrated into all routines during the day.

Case number gym

Numbering skills and learning number symbols are one of the basic areas of mathematics in Finnish Early Childhood Education. Even small children learn reading words by listening and repeating, but number symbols are not often practised with children because pen-and-paper exercises are not part of Finnish Early Childhood Education. In this case, the teacher is guiding an activity where children are practising connecting number names and symbols through a movement-based approach.

In the first excerpt, the teacher was actively directing and guiding children to focus on their spatial awareness and through that to activate their embodiment trough, *bodily learning*. Using the mirror gives children the opportunity to visualise their posture:

> First, the children are asked to stand still like a number 1. The children test and explore different postures until one student comes up with an idea to lift their arms straight upwards. The teacher suggests that everybody tries the posture. The children agree that laughing is the most likely posture they can make. Using the mirror on the wall the teacher helps the children to evaluate the posture from behind and sideways. The children test their muscles by controlling the stomach and back.

In the second excerpt, the teacher combines cognitive learning and memorising the number symbols, with a physically active assignment with movement and directions. However, spatial awareness and control of posture still exist:

> Later on, the teacher introduces the shapes of 2 and 5 by using large cards with the symbol. The children start automatedly to move their bodies to form the curves in the symbols. The teacher points their attention to the direction these symbols are looking at: when number 5 looks forward, number 2 always looks backward. The teacher asks the children to walk or move around the class as 2 or 5 would do, so the children combine the kinaesthetic movement with the posture. Some try to walk on their knees to shape the lower line in 2, but those who have chosen 5 curve their legs.

The teacher is following closely and when they observe the frustration and emotional experiences of the children the teacher focuses on personal feedback and support to scaffold the activity and children's motivation. Through this interaction, the teacher facilitates emotional support and bodily interaction:

> The teacher gives feedback to each child individually. Through the feedback, children get necessary reflection either on the direction

of the movement or the shape of the symbol. The assignment is more difficult than the previous one, so children start complaining. The teacher advises them to straighten their backs and arms again to test how and in which direction number 1 could move. This amuses the children because number 1 cannot walk, it has only one leg.

The described exercise with observation-based understanding seems to help children to connect the symbol with the value through one-to-one correspondence. In the next excerpt, the children accept the support from teachers and invent an activity that the teacher has not planned. The teacher accepts the playful chaos as part of their class plan and is able to implement more kinaesthetic activities relating to this children-initiated idea and introduces a new cognitive concept to them. The children's ideas bring physical activity to the focus of the teacher and she adapts the plan according to the children's needs.

> Soon, number 1s bounce around the class as a result of the students' initiative. The teacher does not have this planned, but sees the opportunity and encourages the rest of the students to join in. Someone suggests number 1 could skip with one foot down and the idea is put into practice. The teacher introduces the concept of 0 who doesn't have any legs. How could it move around? Children curl into little 0 babies on the floor, hugging their knees and spinning around. The teacher scaffolds the students' attention towards the round-shape movement and supports them when a couple of children wish to compare the movement of 0 and 1.

The teacher plans to continue the playful exercise to practise the numbers one to five. Based on their observation of children's ideas and interests, they introduce the concept of zero. When children seem to be actively attached to the action, the teacher changes the plans further and asks for children's opinions and knowledge, as described in the following excerpt where the level of physical activity raises through playfulness.

> The teacher observes the children who spin on the floor practising the concept of zeros laughing and enjoying and asks what would happen if the zero holds hands with another zero. The children soon suggest

that this shape is more like a number eight, and somebody suggests that the number eight (8) looks like a speed running or car track. Children are motivated to test this concept by running, and together with the teacher, they build a track using warning cones, and then children as cars drive through it round after round.

This final excerpt shows how children's active agency through playful learning is strongly connected with kinaesthetic learning experiences. Movement and active embodiment with experienced directions, speed and physicality support children to create concepts of the forms of numbers. Throughout the excerpts, the dimensions of kinaesthetic and embodied learning, *bodily learning, bodily interaction, playful learning and physical activity*, are meaningfully part of the class activity.

Discussion

Finnish ECEC is based on a holistic learning approach where children very often learn through pedagogical projects and continuous learning. Therefore, an active agency and participation are strongly linked with the concepts of learning and development, also in the Finnish ECEC context (Bennett, 2005). In Finland, learning is understood as playful, and it involves embodiment, emotions, communication, and movement through active agency. From these premises, the aim of this chapter was developed. Our aim was to create an overview of the kinaesthetic means of action and communication between teachers and children in ECEC settings in Finland, through the concepts of learning as embodiment and action. This we did with the help of two data sets. With the first data set (curriculum data) we did a systematic content analysis. Here we describe the core concepts and understanding of kinaesthetic, active, and embodied learning, in order to give an overview of the pedagogical practices. With the help of the second data set (a case study) we demonstrated how teachers in ECEC conceptualise and use kinaesthetic learning through embodiment guidance and scaffolding in their classrooms.

Playful learning is constructed through a multidisciplinary understanding of learning as social, cognitive, physical, and active process of interaction. As seen in the analysis considering the curriculum documents from the Finnish

ECEC, this concept of learning is visible also in the guidelines concerning children's physical activity and bodily learning. Children are considered as a whole in education, and thus the conceptions of learning in ECEC pay attention to physical aspects, movement, gestures, spatiality and emotions (see also Johansson et al., 2021; Leinonen & Sintonen, 2014). This requires that teachers of ECEC are aware of learning as a holistic process and have competencies to both support children's learning using embodiment and physical activity, but also know how to plan assignments and classes using these elements in their lesson plans (Johansson et al., 2021). The role of pedagogy can be framed through observation, interaction, support and guidance by the teacher promoting the holistic learning of children (Kangas & Harju-Luukkainen, 2022). Playful pedagogy means also designing and planning educational activities following curriculum goals through multimodal activities and communication (Kangas et al., 2019; Hyvönen & Ruokamo, 2005).

Playfulness and playful pedagogy are methods through which teachers can adopt the physical and embodied approaches of learning as part of their professional competencies and frame the play through modalities of learning and learning through the modalities of play (Kangas & Harju-Luukkainen, 2022). Playful learning contains elements considering extensive experiences, motivation, engagement and process orientation (see Henricks, 1999). In the finding element of having intrinsic rather than extrinsic motives emerged from the case study of number gym, where children were making initiatives about the activities and evolving those. Playful learning also involved active engagement that becomes visible through children's physicality and movement: An excited child cannot sit quietly but shows excitement with their body and emotions.

As shown in this chapter, kinaesthetic learning can be linked with different elements through a holistic and playful approach to learning in Early Childhood Education. Children's active agency through playful learning was strongly connected with kinaesthetic learning experiences where movement and active embodiment with experienced directions, speed and physicality supported children to create concepts and interact around them.

Kinaesthetic learning should not be considered only as sports or physical education when considering the small children in the ECEC services. Meaningful learning through the holistic Early Childhood Education pedagogy is a quality factor of education in the early years. From teachers, it demands an active agency and competence to design and develop pedagogical practices that scaffold children's social awareness and understanding of shared wellbeing. It is linked with sustainable development goals where individuals are participating in society as active citizens.

References

Alila, K., Ukkonen-Mikkola, T., & Kangas, J. (2022). Elements of the pedagogical process in Finnish early childhood education. In H. Harju-Luukkainen, J. Kangas, & S. Garvis (Eds.), *Finnish early childhood education and care: A multi-theoretical perspective on research and practice* (pp. 257–274). Springer International Publishing AG.

Bendelow, G. & Mayall, B. (2002). Children's emotional learning in primary schools. *The European Journal of Psychotherapy, Counselling and Health, 5*(3), 291–304.

Bennett, J. (2005). Curriculum issues in national policy-making. *European Early Childhood Education Research Journal, 13*(2), 5.

Bodrova, E. (2008). Make-believe play versus academic skills: A Vygotskian approach to today's dilemma of early childhood education. *European Early Childhood Education Research Journal, 16*(3), 357–369.

Brooker, L. (2010). Taking play seriously. In S. Rogers (Ed.), *Rethinking play and pedagogy in early childhood education* (pp. 160–172). Routledge.

Denzin, N. & Lincoln, Y. (2000). The disciple and practice of qualitative research. In: Denzin, N. & Y. Lincoln (Eds.), *Handbook of qualitative research*. Second edition (pp. 1–25). Sage Publications.

Dewey, J. (1938). *Logic: A theory of inquiry*. Henry Holt.

DuBose, K. D., Mayo, M. S., Gibson, C. A., Green, J. L., Hill, J. O., Jacobsen, D. J., ... & Donnelly, J. E. (2008). Physical activity across the curriculum (PAAC): Rationale and design. *Contemporary Clinical Trials, 29(1)*, 83–93.

European Commission (1996). *Quality targets in services for young children*. EC Childcare Network, European Commission Equal Opportunities Unit.

Finnish Law of Early Childhood Education 540/2018.

Finnish National Agency for Education (FNAE). (2021). *National Core Curriculum for Two-Year Pre-Primary Education*. EDUFI – Finnish National Agency for Education.

Finnish National Agency for Education (FNAE). (2022). *National Curriculum of Early Childhood Education and Care*. EDUFI – Finnish National Agency for Education.

Finnish National Agency of Education (FNAE). (2014). Opetussuunnitel- man perusteet. Basic Education Core curriculum from www.oph.fi/fi/koulutus-ja-tutkinnot/perusopetuksen-opetussuunnitelmien-perusteet

Hännikäinen, M. (2018). Values of wellbeing and togetherness in the early childhood education of younger children. In E. Johansson & J. Einarsdottir (Eds.), *Values in early childhood education: Citizenship for tomorrow* (pp.147–162). Routledge.

Harju-Luukkainen, H., Garvis, S., & Kangas, J. (2019). "After Lunch We Offer Quiet Time and Meditation": Early learning environments in Australia and Finland through the Lenses of educators. In S. Faas, D. Kasüschke, E. Nitecki, M. Urban, & H. Wasmuth (Eds.), *Globalization, transformation, and cultures in early childhood education and care: Reconceptualization and comparison* (pp. 203–219). Palgrave Macmillan.

Harju-Luukkainen, H., Kangas, J., & Garvis, S. (Eds.) (2022). *Finnish Early childhood education and care: A multi-theoretical perspective on research and practice.* Springer.

Henricks, T. S. (1999). Play as ascending meaning: Implications of a general model of play. In S. Reifel (Ed.), *Play contexts revisited* (pp. 257–277). Ablex Publishing Group.

Hyvönen, P., & Ruokamo, H. (2005). The features of playfulness in the pedagogical model of TPL–tutoring, playing and learning. *Teaching–Studying–Learning (TSL) Processes and Mobile Technologies: Multi-, Inter- and Transdisciplinary, 103.*

Johansson, C., Åberg, M., & Hedlin, M. (2021). Touch the children, or please don't – Preschool teachers' approach to touch. *Scandinavian Journal of Educational Research, 65*(2), 288–301. https://doi.org/10.1080/00313831.2019.1705893

Johnson, M. E. (1999) Embodied reason. In G. Weiss & H. F. Haber (Eds.), *Perspectives on embodiment. The Intersections of nature and culture* (pp. 81–102). Routledge.

Kangas, J., & Harju-Luukkainen, H. (2022). Creating a theoretical framework for playful learning and pedagogy: The Finnish perspective. In H. Harju-Luukkainen, J. Kangas, & S. Garvis (Eds.), *Finnish Early Childhood Education and Care: A Multi-theoretical Perspective on Research and Practice* (pp. 195–208). Springer International Publishing AG.

Kangas, J., Harju-Luukkainen, H., Brotherus, A., Kuusisto, A., & Gearon, L. (2019). Playing to learn in Finland: Early childhood curricular and operational context. In S. Garvis, & S. Phillipson (Eds.), *Policification of Early Childhood Education and Care: Early Childhood Education in the 21st Century Volume III* (pp. 71–85). Routledge

Kangas, J., Ojala, M., & Venninen, T. (2015). Children's self-regulation in the context of participatory pedagogy in early childhood education. *Early Education and Development, 26*, 5–6, 847–870. DOI: 10.1080/10409289.2015.1039434.

Leinonen, J., & Sintonen, S. (2014). Productive participation – Children as active media producers in kindergarten. *Nordic Journal of Digital Literacy, 9*(3), 216–236.

Møller, S. J. (2015). Imagination, playfulness and creativity in children's play with different toys. *American Journal of Play, 7*(3), 322–346.

Moyles, J. R., Stoll, L., & Fink, D. (1989). *Just playing? The role and status of play in early childhood education.* Open University Press.

Neill, S. (2017). *Classroom nonverbal communication.* Routledge.

Price, S., & Rogers, Y. (2004). Let's get physical: The learning benefits of interacting in digitally augmented physical spaces. *Computers & Education, 43*(1–2), 137–151.

Punch, K. F., & Oancea, A. (2014). *Introduction to research methods in education.* Sage Publications.

Rutanen, N. (2012). Socio-spatial practices in a Finnish daycare group for 1 to 3-year-olds. *Early Years: An International Journal of Research and Development 32*(2), 201–214.

Salminen, A. (2011). *Mikä kirjallisuuskatsaus? Johdatus kirjallisuuskatsauksen tyyppeihin ja hallintotieteellisiin sovelluksiin. [What is a literature review? An introduction to the types and applications of literature review in management science].* Vaasan yliopiston julkaisuja.

Sefton-Green, J., Kumpulainen, K., Lipponen, L., Sintonen, S., Rajala, A., & Hilppö, J. (2015). *Playing with learning. The Playful learning center.* University of Helsinki. http://plchelsinki.fi/

Snyder, H. (2019). Literature review as a research methodology: An Overveiw and Guidelines. *Journal of Business Research, 104*, 333–339. https://doi.org/10.1016/j.jbusres.2019.07.039

United Nations Educational, Scientific, and Cultural Organisation (UNESCO). (1989) United Nations. *Convention on the rights of the child.* www.unicef.org/crc/

United Nations Educational, Scientific, and Cultural Organisation (UNESCO). (1994). *The Salamanca statement and framework for action on special needs education.* UNESCO.

United Nations. (1989). *Convention on the rights of the child.* United Nations.

Vartiainen, J. & Kumpulainen, K. (2020). Playing with science: manifestation of scientific play in early science inquiry, *European Early Childhood Education Research Journal.* doi: 10.1080/1350293X.2020.1783924

Whitebread, D., & Basilio, M. (2012). The emergence and early development of self-regulation in young children. *Profesorado, Revista de currículum y formacíon del profesorado, 16*(1), 15–34.

Concluding comments

Susanne Garvis and
Georgina Barton

Introduction

Throughout this book, it has been argued that kinaesthetic learning for young children is crucial for their overall development including physical, psycho-social, emotional and cultural attributes. Indeed, many policies in Early Childhood Education stress the importance of kinaesthetic learning, indicating that a lack of such learning would be detrimental to children's overall health and wellbeing. Consequently, it is the responsibility of Early Years educators, policy makers, parents/carers and families to ensure children experience a range of activities and opportunities involving hands-on and playful learning.

In this concluding chapter we bring together the main themes presented throughout this book and then we turn to recommendations for future research.

Reflections on current understandings of kinaesthetic learning

1. The importance of defining kinaesthetic learning

   In our studies we all found it necessary to define what kinaesthetic learning means so that educators, policy makers etc. have a shared understanding of how to implement kinaesthetic learning in Early Childhood learning contexts. Knowing what kinaesthetic learning

DOI: 10.4324/9781003268772-11

actually is helps educators refine the work they do in different contexts. In Chapter 2 various terms were presented that relate to kinaesthetic learning including digital manipulation, hands-on learning, outdoor learning, physical activity and play. Above all kinaesthetic learning has to involve some kind of active, physical or tactile activity rather than passive learning.

2. The importance of kinaesthetic learning for young children

It was clear that active learning is critical for young children's development. Without kinaesthetic learning there is a risk that children will not grow in areas necessary for holistic development. Kinaesthetic learning is essential for brain development alongside physical, and socio-emotional growth. In addition, kinaesthetic learning can improve children's self-confidence, the ability to work together and their individual capabilities.

3. Educational policy emphasises the importance of kinaesthetic learning in Early Childhood

Across the globe, educational policy highlights the need to include kinaesthetic learning as a basis for all learning for young children. In Australia, for example, the Early Years Learning Framework states that children's learning is complex and dynamic and must include different approaches. Including kinaesthetic learning enables children to develop their sense of identity both independently and guided. It also means that children's wellbeing and resilience is at its utmost best.

4. Approaches to learning and teaching in Early Childhood tend to be teacher-centred

Another theme presented throughout this book is the fact that teachers often feel the pressure to lift assessment scores and hence make approaches to learning and teaching teacher-centred. While some learning admittedly needs to be made explicit with the teacher guiding students it is equally, if not more important, for children to have the space to lead their own learning. Kinaesthetic learning approaches encourage direct participation of children in making decisions about how they learn. Active learning should be privileged over passive learning.

Future research and directions for kinaesthetic learning

In summary, we hope that this book has been useful for all educators, and specifically Early Years educators to consider how to embed kinaesthetic learning in their contexts. In relation to future research and directions we encourage educators to think about how they might be able to conduct small research projects to build a body of evidence-based practice. One way to do this would be to communicate and collaborate with families, with the children's voices at the centre of these discussions. Questions such as:

a. How can we improve the approaches to play in our centre?
b. What types of learning activities do the children prefer?
c. How can we involve the children more in making decisions about kinaesthetic approaches to learning?
d. How can we then measure the impact of these on their overall development?

can be useful in different contexts. Such discussions should be informed by scholarly work, such as the studies presented in this book, alongside educational policies that highlight the importance of active learning for children.

Index

Note: Page numbers in **bold** indicate tables; those in *italics* indicate figures.

For Product Safety Concerns and Information please contact our EU
representative GPSR@taylorandfrancis.com
Taylor & Francis Verlag GmbH, Kaufingerstraße 24, 80331 München, Germany

www.ingramcontent.com/pod-product-compliance
Ingram Content Group UK Ltd.
Pitfield, Milton Keynes, MK11 3LW, UK
UKHW021455080625
459435UK00012B/508